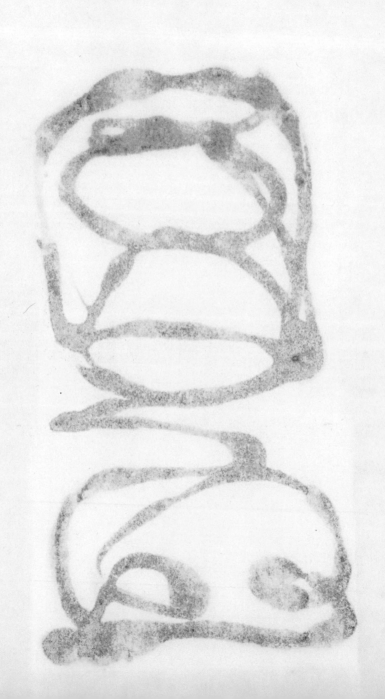

THE MEXICANS IN AMERICA

The IN AMERICA *Series*

THE MEXICANS IN AMERICA

JANE PINCHOT

Published by
Lerner Publications Company
Minneapolis, Minnesota

ACKNOWLEDGMENTS

The illustrations are reproduced through the courtesy of: p. 6, Hyde Park Press; pp. 8, 12, 36, 61, 62, 67, Independent Picture Service; pp. 11, 15, 20, 31, 40, Library of Congress; p. 16, Harwood Advertising, Tucson, Arizona; p. 18, Organization of American States, Pan American Union; p. 25, California Historical Society; p. 27, Wells Fargo Bank, History Room, San Francisco; pp. 28, 70, Arizona Historical Society Library; p. 33, Courtesy of the Detroit Institute of Arts; pp. 34, 50 (left and right), 85 (right), University of Texas, Institute of Texan Cultures; pp. 38, 73, United States Department of Justice, Immigration and Naturalization Service; pp. 43, 49, 57, Wide World Photos; p. 44, Courtesy of Nancy Schreier; pp. 46, 47, Los Angeles Times; p. 53, West Los Angeles Community Service Organization; pp. 54 (left), 85 (left), Office of the Congressmen, Washington, D.C.; p. 54 (right), Courtesy of Juan Cornejo; p. 59 (top left), United States Department of Health, Education, and Welfare, Office of Education; p. 59 (top right), United States Commission on Civil Rights, Washington, D.C.; p. 59 (bottom left), Office of Economic Opportunity, Washington, D.C.; p. 59 (bottom right), United States Department of the Treasury; pp. 64, 81, La Raza Magazine; pp. 68, 77, 78, 88, Religious News Service; pp. 72, 74, Brown Brothers; p. 84, Foreign Service of the United States of America, Paraguay; p. 89, El Grito Del Norte; pp. 90, 91, El Centro Campesino Cultural; p. 92 (left), World Tennis; p. 92 (middle), New England Patriots Football Club; p. 92 (right), Lee Trevino; p. 94, International Famous Agency; p. 95 (left), Barbara Best, Inc.; p. 95 (right), Joan Baez.

LIBRARY OF CONGRESS CATALOGING IN PUBLICATION DATA

Pinchot, Jane.
The Mexicans in America.

(The In America Series)
SUMMARY: A brief history of the Mexicans in the United States — their life in the American Southwest before statehood, the United States acquisition of their land, and the individual contributions of Mexicans to American life.

1. Mexican Americans — Juvenile literature. [1. Mexican Americans] I. Title.

E184.M5P56   301.45'16'872073   72-3587
ISBN 0-8225-0222-4 [Library Edition]
ISBN 0-8225-1016-2 [Paper Edition]

1979 Revised Edition

Copyright ©1979, 1973 by Lerner Publications Company
International Copyright secured. Printed in U.S.A.

International Standard Book Number: 0-8225-0222-4 Library Edition
International Standard Book Number: 0-8225-1016-2 Paper Edition

Library of Congress Catalog Card Number: 72-3587

7   8   9   10   94   93   92   91   90   89   88   87   86   85   84

. . . CONTENTS . . .

Who are the Mexican-Americans?

The Mexican-Americans are a unique people, with a distinctive history and culture. Today most Mexican-Americans live in the southwestern part of the United States. Some of them have emigrated from Mexico in recent years; others are descended from families that have lived in the Southwest since the 16th century. While some Mexican-Americans maintain close ties with Mexico, others have little interest in the affairs of that nation. Some Mexican-Americans live in communities with people of the same heritage; others live where few, if any, people have a similar background. Furthermore, some Mexican-Americans speak only Spanish, some only English, and others a combination of the two languages.

Reflecting these differences, various segments of the Mexican-American community have come to prefer different names. While many wish to be called "Mexican-Americans," others argue that the hyphen is unnecessary. At the same time, some prefer the names "Latin-Americans," "Spanish-Americans," "Hispanic-Americans," or "Chicanos." Others feel that they should simply be called "Americans," without the addition of another word.

Despite such differences in attitude, background, and way of life, the members of the Mexican-American community are united by the proud heritage that they share. The story of that heritage and of the Mexican-American experience in the United States is presented in the following pages.

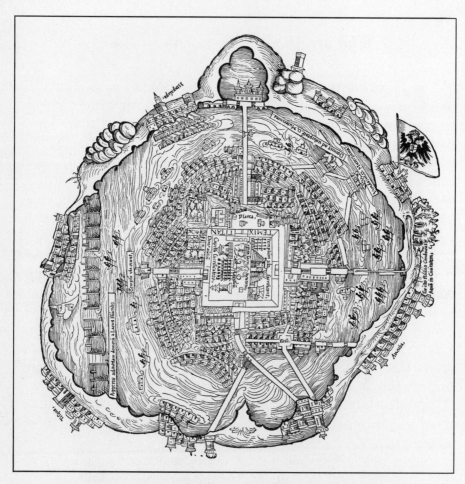

The island city of Tenochtitlán, capital of the Aztec empire. This 16th-century map, supposedly drawn by **Hernan Cortes**, shows the city's broad causeways and its impressive main square.

PART I

The Origin of the American Southwest

1. *Two Worlds Meet*

Until the 16th century, the two peoples who became the ancestors of the Mexican-Americans lived on separate continents. The Spaniards of Europe and the Indians of Middle America were unaware of each other's culture and unaffected by each other's existence.

In the early 16th century, the Aztec Indians dominated the area of Middle America which later became Mexico. The Aztecs had a highly developed civilization that differed in many ways from the civilization of 16th-century Europe. Religion and warfare were among the most important elements in Aztec life. The Indians believed that their gods controlled all aspects of life, from the daily rising and setting of the sun to the outcome of the battles they fought to maintain control of their empire. When the Aztecs engaged in warfare, they did not kill their opponents on the battlefield. Instead, the Indians attempted to capture enemies so that they could be offered as sacrifices to the gods.

Despite this emphasis on war, the values and the social structure of the Aztec civilization centered around the family and the community. People won prestige by serving the community, and honor was considered an extremely important personal quality.

The capital of the Aztec empire, Tenochtitlán, was one of the largest and most sophisticated cities of the early 16th century. Located on an island in a shallow lake, the city had great temple pyramids, aqueducts which carried clean water, barbershops, parks, and a zoo. As capital of the empire, Tenochtitlán was the home of Moctezuma II, emperor of the Aztecs.

On the other side of the Atlantic, Queen Isabella and King Ferdinand of Spain ruled over a kingdom which had only recently been united after centuries of turmoil. In 1492 Isabella had sponsored the first voyage of Christopher Columbus and, following his discovery, had laid claim to most of the unseen lands of the New World. The Spanish rulers saw the Americas as a source of riches and as an opportunity to extend the influence of the Roman Catholic Church, the official church of Spain. Therefore, they encouraged men to seek wealth and to win conversions to Catholicism in the distant land.

Among those who accepted this challenge was a young Spanish explorer and adventurer, Hernan Cortes. In 1519 Cortes sailed from the Spanish island of Cuba, bound for the coast of Mexico. Sighting his vessels, the Aztecs warned Moctezuma that "strange men, riding in white-winged ships," were approaching from the eastern sea. The emperor, a deeply religious man, took this announcement to mean that the prophecy of an ancient Aztec legend was being fulfilled. According to the legend, the god Quetzalcoatl had left centuries before, promising to return from the eastern sea in the year of the Aztec calendar corresponding to 1519. To please the returning god, Moctezuma sent men to greet the landing ships and to shower the Spaniards with gifts of gold.

When Cortes realized that the Aztecs possessed an abundance of gold, he was determined to conquer their empire. To help him devise a plan of attack, he enlisted the aid of other Indian tribes in the area. The most valuable assistance came from a young Indian girl named Malinche, who served as an interpreter and informer. Malinche helped Cortes persuade the Totonac and Tlaxcalan tribes to become his allies. Eager to be rid of their Aztec rulers, the tribes joined the European soldiers.

When Cortes and his allies arrived in Tenochtitlán, they quickly gained control. Moctezuma, who still believed Cortes to be Quetzalcoatl, welcomed the Spanish soldiers, gave them a palace to live in, and agreed to convert to Catholicism. Cortes accepted this welcome to the city and allowed Moctezuma to continue ruling the empire.

The emperor **Moctezuma** welcomes Cortes to Tenochtitlán.

The peace was soon broken, however, when Spanish soldiers killed Aztec noblemen to gain possession of their gold. The people of the city protested the Spaniards' brutality, and when Moctezuma tried to appease them, he himself was killed. The people of Tenochtitlán then turned against the Spaniards and forced them to flee the city. Many Spaniards and Indians met death on this night of violence, later known as *La Noche Triste* (The Sad Night).

While the Spaniards regrouped and regained their strength outside the city, the Indians within Tenochtitlán encountered their deadliest enemies—smallpox and influenza. These two diseases were unknown in the Americas until the Europeans brought them over from the Old World. By 1521, when Cortes and his men again invaded the island city, the Indians had been greatly weakened by epidemics of the European diseases. But the Aztecs were warriors, and they fought valiantly to defend their homeland. They managed to hold out for three months against their attackers, despite the odds against them. The island was surrounded by Spanish ships, and the aqueducts supplying fresh water to the city had been cut. The Aztec warriors were

This Indian drawing shows the Spanish assault on Tenochtitlán in 1521. At the top, Cortes, accompanied by the Indian girl Malinche, approaches the island city by boat. Below, Malinche and two Spanish soldiers confront a group of Aztec warriors.

armed only with primitive weapons against the Spaniards' guns, and they were weakened by hunger and foreign disease. But Cuauhtemoc, the new Aztec emperor, had pledged to fight to the death of the last Aztec soldier. Only after the capture of Cuauhtemoc did the Aztecs admit defeat.

After Tenochtitlán fell to Cortes and his men, drastic changes began to take place in the Aztec empire. By 1607, smallpox, measles, and influenza had decreased the Indian population by 90 to 95 percent. With the number of Indians so greatly reduced, the Spaniards were easily able to control the entire empire.

Other changes also affected the population of the Spanish territory, now called New Spain. Many of the men sent to settle and protect the colony took Indian wives and mistresses. The children of these unions were called *mestizos*, meaning "mixed blood." In a short time, this new racial group outnumbered both the full-blooded Spaniards and Indians in New Spain.

Changes also took place in the religious life of the country. Roman Catholicism was made the official religion of New Spain, just as in Spain itself. But the Indians of the New World preserved some of the beliefs and practices of their old religion and combined them with the new faith taught by the Spanish missionaries. A distinctive feature of this combined religion originated in 1531, when a young Indian boy, Juan Diego, saw a vision of an Indian maiden at a site where the temple of an Aztec goddess once stood. The maiden called herself Holy Mary of Guadalupe and requested that a church be built in her honor. Designated saint and holy mother by the Catholic Church, the Virgin of Guadalupe became the patron saint of Mexico and helped to give the Mexican people a religion that combined their Indian background with European Catholicism.

Other changes in the way of life in Mexico were brought about by the Spaniards' introduction of domestic animals, such as the horse and the sheep, and by their creation of a new social class system. The highest social class in New Spain consisted of *peninsulares*, or Spaniards born in Spain, who controlled the country. The next class consisted of *criollos*—Spaniards born in America —followed by the mestizos. The lowest class was made up of the full-blooded Indians. At times the Indians and mestizos were used as slaves or employed as servants in a system called debt peonage. This system provided that, in order to repay a debt, a man could be held in bondage for his lifetime; his decendants could also be held responsible for the debt.

2. *Pioneers of the Southwest*

Only a few years after Cortes had conquered Mexico, the people of New Spain began to explore what is today the Southwest of the United States. At first many of them went in search of gold.

One of the first Spaniards to travel in the Southwest was Alvar Núñez Cabeza de Vaca. After being shipwrecked on the coast of Florida, Cabeza de Vaca traveled to Mexico City on foot. When he arrived in 1536, he reported an Indian legend he had heard which told of the existence of seven cities of gold, called the Seven Cities of Cíbola. Cabeza de Vaca's tale was responsible for stirring up much excitement about the unfamiliar territory north of Mexico.

In 1539, a black Moroccan named Estevan, who had accompanied Cabeza de Vaca, and a Catholic priest, Fray (Father) Marcos de Niza, set out to search for the cities of gold. Together they explored the Indian lands now part of New Mexico and Arizona, claiming the territory for Spain and the Catholic Church. Following the murder of Estevan by Zuñi tribesmen, Father Marcos returned to Mexico City and reported that he had glimpsed the legendary cities.

Stirred by Father Marcos' report, another Spaniard set out to find wealth in the Southwest. Francisco Vásquez de Coronado, accompanied by 300 Spaniards and 300 Indians, explored the land from 1540 through 1542. Coronado and his companions discovered and claimed for Spain the territories later known as lower California, Arizona, New Mexico, and the Texas and Oklahoma panhandles. However, they failed to find the seven cities and, disappointed, returned to Mexico.

A fourth explorer, Juan de Oñate, established the first enduring colony in the Southwest. After leaving Mexico in 1595, Oñate's expedition settled in New Mexico and founded the *pueblo*, or community, of Sante Fe. The party of settlers was diverse, including families, soldiers, and missionaries; Spaniards, Negroes, Indians, and mestizos. By 1630, at least 25 missions and 90 pueblos were established on land that would eventually become the states of Texas, New Mexico, Utah, Colorado, Kansas, and Nebraska. After existing peaceably with the northern Indians for 50 years, these early settlements vanished during the revolt of the Pueblo Indians in 1680. Only the people of Sante Fe survived, and they soon retreated to the outpost of El Paso.

Following the Pueblo revolt, the government of Spain instituted a three-part settlement system, each part of which served a separate function. The three elements of the system were the pueblo, the community of settlers; the *presidio*, a military fort staffed with soldiers for defense of the pueblo; and the mission, a church whose job it was to convert and teach the Indians. Settlements based on this system were again attempted in the late 17th century. A small force of Spaniards, Indians, and mestizos left El Paso in 1692 under the leadership of Diego de

Vargas. The 800 settlers recolonized the area of New Mexico and restored 23 of the pueblos there.

Fear of Indian attack caused many settlements to be abandoned in the years that followed. Then, in the 18th century, Spain again encouraged settlements, motivated by a desire to protect Spanish-claimed lands from invasions by other European countries. The nation which had once claimed the right to almost all of the New World lands now felt that her remaining claims were being threatened by France, Russia, and Great Britain.

To prevent French movement from Louisiana into the Texas area, four presidios and 10 missions were created in Texas between 1715 and 1730. A few years after the French threat ceased, Russia presented cause for concern. To keep Russian settlements in California from spreading, Fray Junípero Serra started Franciscan missions in the California area. In 1769, Spain was warned that Great Britain also posed a threat in California. José Gálvez, sent to New Spain by the king, believed that a

This statue of the Spanish missionary **Junípero Serra** stands in Statuary Hall in the United States Capitol.

San Xavier del Bac, near Tucson, was one of the early
Spanish missions established in the Southwest.

stronger base was needed in California to protect the region.
Therefore, he called for the founding of missions and presidios
both at Monterey and at San Diego.

By the year 1770, Spain had settlements throughout the
California, New Mexico, and Texas regions. Most of these settlements were led by peninsulares or criollos, but the vast majority
of pioneers were Indians and mestizos. The Indians were usually
employed as servants—mule drivers, packers, and camp attend-
ants. The more numerous group, the mestizos, came to find
opportunity and a new life. Unable to gain prestige in Mexico
because of their low status, these people could become soldiers
and subordinate officials in the new territories.

At the end of the Hispanic, or Spanish, era, the important settlements in the Southwest were Laredo, San Antonio, and El Paso
in Texas; Sante Fe in New Mexico; Tucson and Tubac in Arizona;
and San José in California, with Los Angeles and San Diego small
but growing in importance. Due to the great distances which
separated them, each of these early settlements was isolated both
from Mexico City and from the other colonies. Roads were few,
and the main contact with other communities was provided by
the mule trains and the *carretas* (wagons) that carried goods from

Mexico City. Spanish law forbidding trade with foreigners kept the settlers from mingling with people from other countries.

But life in the early pueblos was in many ways like the life of Hispanic communities in other places. The missions, for example, were extremely important in territorial life. They owned herds, flocks, orchards, vineyards, fields, and workshops. Native Indians provided much of the labor used in the mission fields.

Other distinguishing features of life in the settlements of New Spain were the so-called pueblo laws which governed them. These laws were based on a concept of community ownership that dated back to the laws of the ancient Romans. Water rights and mineral rights were owned by the entire community rather than by individuals. The concept of community ownership also affected the property laws of the early pueblos. The central plaza in each town, for instance, was owned by the entire community and benefited everyone. Personal property was owned by family units rather than by individuals.

Today, laws based on the old pueblo laws allow the state and federal governments to control the main waterways and the subsoil rights in the Southwest. Current community property laws such as those in California are also based on old pueblo laws. These laws assume that the property owned by a married couple, for example, belongs to them jointly. If they divorce, each can claim half of the property.

3. *New Governments for the Southwest*

While the people of the Southwest were struggling to survive in their independent communities, events were occurring in Europe that would cause the area to be ruled by three different governments in less than half a century. The chain of events that altered the course of history in the Southwest began in 1808 with the invasion of Spain by Napoleon Bonaparte of France. After his conquest of Spain, Napoleon placed his brother Joseph on the Spanish throne.

Up to this time, New Spain had always been considered the personal property of Spain's ruling monarch. The land was thought to be directly inherited from Queen Isabella, who had financed Columbus' journey to the New World. However, when the king of Spain was dethroned and replaced by Joseph Bonaparte, people in New Spain questioned the mother country's right to continue to rule over them. Those who were especially discontented with Spain's policies began to work for change. The criollos wanted rights and powers equal to those of the peninsulares. Others, led by Father Miguel Hidalgo y Costilla, wanted equality for all classes. In 1810 Hidalgo's cry for "land, liberty, justice, and equality" set off feuds and battles throughout Mexico. Chaos continued until all of the groups joined together to proclaim the independence of Mexico in 1821.

Father Miguel Hidalgo y Costilla,
the Father of Mexican Independence

Although the effects of independence were not immediate, the new government of Mexico established three policies that would eventually create drastic and lasting changes in the life of the Southwest: the rich mission lands were divided into private ranches; trade restrictions were eased; and Anglo-Americans were allowed to settle in Mexican territory.

After the Mexican revolution the church lost some of its power in Mexico, and its valuable land holdings were divided. Part of the mission lands in the Southwest were turned into large ranches and given to individuals by the Mexican governors. Community holdings for grazing were also formed out of the mission lands to be used by those who, in the Spanish tradition, owned livestock but no property. While the amounts of land granted were large, specific boundaries were rarely described. (This custom presented no problem so long as the Southwest was under Mexican rule, but it was later to cause great difficulty when the area became part of the United States.)

With the creation of the large ranches came some of the Southwest's richest traditions. The colorfully dressed *rancheros* (ranch owners), with their wives and large families, worked mainly to achieve what was most important to them—the leisure to enjoy life. They delighted in long conversations with pleasant company, a long meal with the family, dancing, and relaxation. Most of the major events of frontier life were celebrated with popular dances—the contradanze, the jarraba, and the fandango. Fiestas were held to celebrate weddings, births, political changes, and religious holidays.

Along with the creation of the large ranches came the *vaquero*, who became the model for the later cowboy of the Southwest. On Mexican ranches the vaqueros herded cattle, developed ranching techniques and equipment, and exhibited their skills at rodeos. These early ranch hands were also responsible for devising the practical costume worn by later cowboys, as well as the western saddle.

The Mexican government's policy of dividing mission lands made possible the development of the ranching tradition in the Southwest. A second government policy that changed the Southwest was the lessening of trade restrictions, which enabled foreign traders to enter Mexican lands legally. The Southwesterners welcomed the first Anglo-Americans, who brought with them goods to trade. Arriving in small numbers, many of the traders stayed in Mexican territory, adopted the Hispanic way of life, learned the Spanish language, and converted to Roman Catholicism. Some married Mexican women and started families.

Mexican policy also allowed Anglo-American settlers to enter the territory of the Southwest and establish communities there. The first organized Anglo settlement in Mexican territory was started by Stephen Austin, who in 1821 led 300 families to form

The town of Austin was established in 1823 by Anglo settlers in Texas.

a colony in Texas. These families, like the Anglo traders, adopted Mexican traditions, converted to Catholicism, and became citizens of Mexico. Mexicanos and Anglos existed at peace together so long as only a few Anglos had settled on Mexican lands. But cultural conflicts developed as more and more settlers entered the territory.

Texas was the first to feel the effects of a mass entry of Anglo-Americans. In an area where only 4,000 settlers had lived in 1820, some 20,000 Americans had settled by 1832, and another 10,000 by 1836. Many of these settlers brought slaves with them, in violation of Mexican law. These newcomers had little desire to adapt to the culture of their new home.

Large numbers of Anglo-American invaders also arrived in California. As in Texas, the newcomers created massive problems. When they arrived they agreed to become citizens of Mexico and to convert to the national religion, but they were often hostile to the Mexican way of life. Some of them moved onto lands controlled by Mexicans and raised crops in competition with the native Californians.

Conflict between the Anglos and the Mexicanos in the Southwest reached its first peak in Texas. The *Tejanos* (native Texans) felt their homeland was being invaded by disrespectful foreigners. The Anglos, on the other hand, believed they were morally and intellectually superior to the citizens of their new country. They did not understand the established chain of command in the settlements and often ignored it. Unfamiliar with the idea of working primarily in order to enjoy life, the ambitious newcomers interpreted the Mexican work ethic as a sign of laziness. Protestant settlers practiced their religion in violation of Mexican law and openly expressed their view that those who followed the national religion were fanatic, bigoted, and superstitious. The Mexican system of justice, based on Roman law, was also strange to the Americans, who were used to a system based on English common law.

There were other aspects of Hispanic life not easily understood by the Anglo-Americans. The extreme importance of the family seemed strange to them, as did the debt bondage system, wherein a debtor and his sons could be held in bondage for their lifetimes. They could not distinguish between this system and slavery, which was illegal under Mexican law. But perhaps least understood was the respect for *personalissmo* that existed in the Southwest. While the Anglo-Americans had great respect for institutions, the people of Hispanic cultures viewed individuals as more important than institutions. One consequence of this attitude was that the government of Mexico changed policy with each man who served as its head. The Americans felt that a strong, stable institution was superior to such a changing, individualistic government.

When Antonio López de Santa Anna took office as president of Mexico in 1832, the Anglo-Americans expected that the new government would become similar to the government of the United States. Santa Anna, however, soon disappointed them. He demanded that the Texans pay all Mexican taxes and rid the area of illegal slaves. In addition, he sent troops to Texas to back up his demands that the people obey the laws of their new country.

Insisting on what they considered their rights, the Texans took up arms and seized the Alamo, a military garrison in San Antonio. Santa Anna declared their act a rebellion and laid siege to their stronghold. After defeating the Texans at the Alamo, Santa Anna and his troops proceeded to San Jacinto. There victory went to the Texans, who, under Sam Houston, made a surprise attack on the Mexican forces. Santa Anna was captured, only to regain his freedom by signing a treaty that proclaimed the independence of Texas. This document, however, was not honored by Mexico because of the circumstances under which it was signed.

The United States government was divided on what to do about Texas. But in 1845 Congress resolved the matter (and prepared the way for the Mexican-American War) by issuing a Joint Resolution calling for the annexation of Texas as far south as the Rio Grande River. To enforce this claim, U.S. troops were sent to the Rio Grande. Mexico sent troops across the river to defend territory she still considered her own, and a battle ensued. The United States then used the claim that Mexicans had shed American blood on American soil as an excuse to declare war on Mexico.

Although some fighting took place in California, New Mexico, and Texas, most of the war was fought in Mexico. Generals Zachary Taylor and Winfield Scott engaged in battle strategies aimed at conquering Mexico City. To meet this challenge, Santa Anna took personal command of the Mexican army. Although the well-trained U.S. troops defeated the recently organized Mexican troops in a number of battles, the United States was not able to force Mexico to admit defeat. An attempt was then made to settle the war in a peace conference. The United States proposed an armistice and offered Santa Anna a $10,000 bribe to send a representative to the conference. Santa Anna accepted the bribe and sent an envoy to the conference—but instructed him not to sign anything. After this failure the war resumed. In 1847 General Scott took Mexico City, and Santa Anna was forced to resign the presidency. The following year, the United States was able to negotiate a treaty with the new government that ended the war.

The Treaty of Guadalupe-Hidalgo ended the conflict between Mexico and the United States, but it created many more problems than it solved. By the terms of the treaty, one-third of Mexico was transferred to the United States. The inhabitants of the transferred territory were given U.S. citizenship and were promised protection from hostile Indians who lived in the area. However, Americans did not always respect the rights of the new citizens. Property rights were ignored, and Indians continued to raid Mexican land. In addition, because the boundaries established by the treaty had been based on a faulty map, both countries still claimed the same territory.

Both to correct the mistakes of the treaty and to obtain land for the expansion of its railroads, the United States negotiated the Gadsden Purchase in 1854. The purchase transferred even more Mexican land to the United States. By the middle of the 19th century, the United States had gained control of territory that would eventually become the states of Texas, California, Arizona, Colorado, and New Mexico. Before this time, Mexico had been considerably larger than the United States, but now the situation was reversed.

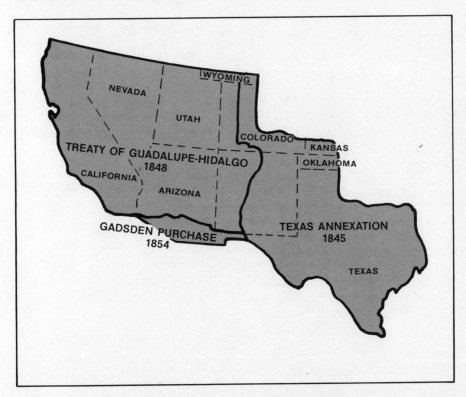

Territory lost by Mexico in the 19th century

PART II

A Conquered People

1. *The Other Side of Progress*

When the United States added the Southwest to its territory, it acquired not only the land but also the people who lived on the land and their cultural heritage. Gradually, Anglo-Americans adopted much of what was useful in that heritage. Spanish and Indian words which became part of the English language include such familiar words as *poncho, cafeteria, bonanza, canyon, corral, fiesta, marina, pronto, tornado, alligator, avocado, banana, tomato, barbecue,* and *chocolate*. Spanish names for rivers, mountains, and cities were also used by the Americans. The distinctive style of architecture found in the Southwest—the one-story ranch house and buildings with tiled roofs, adobe walls, patios, and verandas—was created by Hispanic people and later adopted by Anglo-Americans.

The United States also profited from the economic development of the Southwest. The Mexican ranching culture became a part of American life: breeds of sheep and cattle, ranching techniques, irrigation systems, and methods of weaving wool were borrowed from the Mexican people. Mexican discoveries of gold and quicksilver laid the base for the future development of American mining in the southwestern states. Mines that had been opened in the Mexican era and closed during the Mexican-

24

American War were reclaimed afterward by Anglo-American prospectors. Drawing on the knowledge gained from 200 years of mining, the Mexicans introduced the Anglo-Americans to the equipment needed for mining in the arid lands of the Southwest. They showed them how to use a flat-bottomed bowl with sloping sides, called a *batea*, to pick up rocks for examination, and the *arrastra*, a round stone which pulverized rocks.

Mexicans introduced Anglo-American miners to the *arrastra*, a device used to crush ore-bearing rock.

The Mexican people brought many valuable gifts to their new nation, but Anglo-Americans did not often appreciate their contributions. Instead of being welcomed, the new American citizens were feared and hated. The Treaty of Guadalupe-Hidalgo had promised the Mexican-Americans full citizenship and property rights, but the promise was not kept. From the beginning, Mexican people of the Southwest were the objects of prejudice because of their race, their religion, and their culture.

Racial prejudice colored many of the events that took place in the Southwest. It led Anglo-Americans to accuse Mexicans of being cowardly, cruel, lazy, and corrupt. The language barrier was another source of serious problems between the Anglos and the Mexicanos. Although the first Anglos in the Southwest adapted easily to the Spanish language, later groups distrusted those who spoke any language other than English. Since the United States had acquired the land, many Anglos assumed they had the right to impose their language on all of its inhabitants. Laws came to be written only in English, leaving Spanish-speaking people ignorant of the law. Later, testifying in court in Spanish became illegal. Soon schools were forbidden to allow Spanish to be spoken in the classroom.

Land losses added to the miseries of the conquered people. Despite the fact that the Treaty of Guadalupe-Hidalgo had promised to protect their property rights, most Mexican ranchers lost their lands. Land reform laws were passed which demanded that all lands be measured and that owners file claims to their lands with the United States government. The new laws put the burden of proving claims on the landowners, and many Mexican-Americans lost land that had been granted to them by the Mexican government because they could not show proof of exact boundaries. (Setting up exact boundaries was not considered necessary under Mexican law.) Other landowners lost territory because they could not show written proof of grants made to their families centuries before.

Other changes also robbed the Mexican-Americans of their livelihood. In Texas, barbed wire fences forced ranchers who owned cattle but did not own land to discontinue their customary way of life. California's gold rush forced landowners off their own property; gold seekers from the East camped on the ranch lands, not understanding the need for vast expanses on which to graze cattle. As the squatters became numerous, the rancheros were powerless to fight them. Later, natural disasters completed the displacement of Mexican-Americans. Floods and droughts in the 1880s and 1890s destroyed small farms, causing them to be abandoned.

As a result of these combined hardships, the Mexican-Americans of the 19th century lost their land, their economic independence, and their status. They were often gunned, lynched, captured, and jailed without cause. Feared for their differences, they were segregated completely. Though they worked with Anglo-Americans, the Mexicanos lived separately, using different schools and places of recreation, worship, and even burial.

While most Mexicans accepted their fate in order to survive in the Southwest, a few rebelled against the injustices they saw affecting their people. Among these folk heroes were Joaquin Murieta, Tiburcio Vasquez, and Juan Cortina. Murieta led raids in the 1850s which were so feared that the California legislature commissioned the Texas Rangers to capture him. Vasquez fought the Anglos in his own way during the years from 1852 to 1875. By means of robbery and cattle rustling, he attempted to avenge the abuses suffered by the Mexican-Americans. During the 1860s, Cortina, the "Red Robber of the Rio Grande," also declared war on the enemies of his people. Despite their failure to turn the tide of events, these outlaws were supported by poor Mexican-Americans who had become powerless in the Southwest.

Joaquin Murieta

The 19th century was a period of loss for the Mexican-Americans, but it was a time of prosperity for the Southwest in general. During the era that followed the Mexican-American War, Anglos built communities and industries, rapidly expanding the economy and population of the Southwest. Mines came to be scattered throughout the area, beginning with the California gold rush in 1849. Colorado grew with the discovery of silver in 1859; Arizona became populated with the discoveries of copper, silver, and zinc in the 1870s; by 1900, copper, silver, and zinc were found in New Mexico, and salt mining was established in Texas.

The first new agricultural crop in the American Southwest was cotton, brought to Texas before the Civil War. The growth of agriculture in the area was aided by the Reclamation Act of 1902, which provided a source of water that enabled large produce farms to survive. Finally, the railroad supplied the means for shipping the products of the expanding industries, increased the available markets, and became a growing industry in its own right.

At first, laws kept Mexicans from working in the mines, slaves tended the cotton, and Oriental workers picked the produce and worked on the railroads. But the scene soon changed; slavery was abolished in 1865, the Chinese Exclusion Act of

Mexican workers like these miners at an Arizona copper mine played an important role in the economic development of the Southwest.

1882 restricted the importation of Chinese laborers, and the Gentlemen's Agreement of 1902 reduced the number of Japanese workers.

By 1910 the Southwest had a great need for additional laborers. Events taking place in Mexico made it possible for Mexican workers to fill this need. In 1910, a revolution ousted President Porfirio Díaz from office and put an end to the debt-bondage system. The years following the overthrow of Díaz were filled with chaos and terror in Mexico. Over 1 million people were killed in the civil war between 1910 and 1925. Homes, crops, and livestock were destroyed. Typhus spread. During these years, thousands of Mexican peasants, freed from the debt-bondage system, came north to escape the horror and poverty of life in Mexico.

Three industries—railroads, agriculture, and mining—recruited, supported, and determined the life-style of almost all the Mexicans who migrated north in the early years of the 20th century. These industries kept their new wage laborers separated from the mainstream of activity in the Southwest. Housed in labor camps and cheap housing near the work sites, the Mexican workers were nearly always isolated physically, socially and politically. Thus, they had little opportunity to become part of the main culture.

The railroads not only served as a means of transportation from Mexico but also as a principle employer of Mexican labor in the United States. Most Mexican immigrants in the early years of the 20th century worked for the railroads at some time. Use of this labor force began in the 1880s, when the Southern Pacific and Sante Fe lines hired Mexican workers for construction, particularly in the desert sections. Mexicans also worked at repairing and maintaining the western rail lines. Watchmen of the rails and section men who needed to live near their work were often housed in boxcars roughly adapted for human occupation. Wherever these cars were located for a period of time, a small *colonia*, or colony, soon appeared. These settlements of rough shacks along the rail lines were the beginnings of many of today's Mexican-American communities.

Agricultural interests also encouraged migrations from Mexico to provide the hand labor needed to pick the cotton, fruit, vegetable, and sugar beet crops. Cotton growers in Texas were the first agricultural employers of Mexican labor. In 1910, the first cotton was planted in the Imperial Valley in California. The event coincided with the Mexican revolution, and the Imperial Valley soon became a popular destination for Mexicans who were part of the great migration. In the next 10 years, other areas in the Southwest irrigated and began planting cotton. The Mesilla Valley in New Mexico, the Gila and Salt River valleys in Arizona, and the San Joaquin Valley in central California, all began intensive production of cotton.

Other agricultural crops soon joined cotton as big business in the Southwest. The growing of melons, grapes, citrus fruits, and vegetables required a large initial investment, first to irrigate the land, then to pay for brush clearing, deep plowing, leveling, and extensive planting. Moreover, there was often a long wait for the first crop. This great expenditure left little capital for growers to spend on the labor needed to plant, tend, and harvest the crops. Growers soon depended upon the Mexican labor force for the care of the crops. The need for labor was kept high as improved technology—in the form of perfected boxcars, home refrigerators, and better canning methods—expanded the market for perishable fruits.

Sugar beet growers also recruited workers from Mexico. Initially employing other immigrant groups, they switched to Mexican labor after the Immigration Act of 1924 halted the inflow of other immigrants. El Paso, Texas, became the principal place of recruitment for sugar beet workers in the Rocky Mountain states, while San Antonio served as the recruitment center for the Middle West. In many areas, Mexicans harvested the crop along a migratory route, journeying from one field to another to pick the beets. When growers decided that they needed a permanent work force, however, they sometimes used coercion to fill their need. By refusing to pay the final wages to their workers, the growers could acquire a captive force that lacked the funds to leave the area.

Mexican laborers pick cantaloupes in California's Imperial Valley during the early years of the 20th century.

Working the fields provided a way of life for every member of the family, regardless of age or sex. All members, from the very young to the elderly, were relied upon to contribute to the family's income. Though fast and experienced workers could earn good wages at the height of the season by spending 12 to 14 hours a day in the field, the peak season only lasted part of the year. The income, however, had to last for the whole year, through a winter in which there was often no work available at all. Many migrants became trapped in a cycle of poverty, forced into debt when their summer earnings ran out. Living conditions for the people who engaged in "stoop labor" were usually extremely poor. Sometimes no sanitary facilities were provided nearby, and drinking water was unavailable in the fields. Workers usually lived in housing provided by the growers, often a shack of one or two rooms for the entire family, with no electricity, plumbing, or cooking facilities.

A third employer of Mexican labor in the Southwest during the early 20th century was the mining industry. Copper, ore, and coal mining were expensive operations. Only industrial giants could afford to build the necessary water plants, crushing mills, smelters, and railroads needed for production. In fact, so much wealth was necessary to finance each mine that even industrial giants felt a need for inexpensive labor. Thus they looked to Mexico for their workers; coal mines in Colorado and New Mexico, ore mines in Colorado and Arizona, and smelters in Arizona provided employment for many Mexican laborers. Mexican employees of the mines lived in settlements that ordinarily consisted of rude adobe huts outside the town limits.

During the First World War a portion of the Mexican-American community began to leave the three usual fields of employment. War industries provided jobs and high wages for the Mexican-Americans who learned skilled trades Workers also began to move farther north to find employment, for the first time leaving their historic homeland. Many left because of competition with newcomers from Mexico who were willing to accept jobs for lower wages than the native Americans. The Mexican-Americans who could not live on those low wages moved north where wages were higher and where they could take advantage of being able to speak English. Soon they held jobs as coremakers, machinists, and mechanics in metal and machinery factories; as finishers and upholsterers in wood manufacturing; as mechanics and painters in chemical, oil, and paint industries; as bookbinders, and photo and job press workers in printing and paper industries. Mexican-Americans also worked in the meat packing plants and steel mills of Ohio and Pennsylvania.

By the end of the 1920s the image of agricultural worker no longer fit all Mexican-Americans. The move north, the industrial opportunities of the First World War, and the creation of a skilled working class contributed to making this image less valid.

During the 1920s, many Mexican-Americans moved to the northern states to seek employment. Some of them found jobs working on industrial assembly lines like the one pictured in this mural by Mexican artist Diego Rivera.

2. An "Alien" Population

During the 1920s, the era of the great migration from Mexico, thousands of Mexican immigrants came to the United States seeking better jobs and better lives. Despite the stereotype which Anglos often applied to Mexican-Americans, these newcomers were not all peons, or peasant farmers. Members of the upper classes also crossed the United States-Mexican border. Many of them moved north to escape the civil war in Mexico or to seek business and educational opportunities. These upper-class Mexicans were readily accepted into society and had little trouble adapting to their new lives, though occasionally they were hampered by being associated with their lower-class countrymen.

A different story describes the fate of the Mexican peons who became wage laborers in the United States. Their move north was prompted both by their desire for opportunity and the desire of American businessmen for workers. Fleeing the ravages of war and the prospect of starvation in Mexico, some came to the United States in the hope of settling permanently. Others came

Many Mexican peons came to the United States in
the 1920s seeking a better life for their families.

hoping to save enough money to support their families when they
returned to Mexico. Some men worked in the United States in
order to send funds for the support of relatives left behind.

For the Mexican, crossing the border seldom involved the
commitment to a new way of life that characterized the migration
of the European immigrant. Instead, most Mexicans viewed the
Southwest as a part of their own country, settled by their ancestors, where many of their people still lived and worked. When
they arrived, the newcomers usually entered communities where
they could live and work alongside others who spoke their
language and shared their heritage.

For many years United States policies encouraged this informal
attitude toward migrations from Mexico. So few restrictions
barred the paths of those who wished to cross the border that
the United States neither viewed the moves as immigrations
nor counted the number of immigrants. This outlook held by
both the Anglos and the Mexicans reflected the situation existing
along the border for over half a century. Until the first decades
of the 20th century, disputes and chaos prevailed along the un-
natural international boundary, making attempts to regulate
northbound traffic impossible.

When the area began to calm down, the undesirability of restriction gained importance over the impossibility. The Southwest was growing so rapidly during this era that a large number of laborers from Mexico could be absorbed into the economy without matching the growing demand. So many workers were needed that the Contract Labor Law was suspended from 1918 to 1921. (This law, dating from 1885, forbade American employers to hire laborers in other countries for work in the United States.) During the three-year period, over 50,000 workers were recruited in Mexico to help fill the labor shortage. The United States also extended an "open-door" policy to most other countries, making possible unrestricted immigration. The major exceptions to this policy were China and Japan. Ironically, it was to prevent Oriental laborers from entering the United States by way of Mexico that the first border patrol was established in 1904. The patrols took no notice of the Mexican laborers who traveled north to fill positions left vacant by Orientals.

The first restrictions of Mexican migrations came when border stations were established to arrange for admissions, to record the number of entrants, and to collect a head tax from each person who wished to immigrate. Although no restrictions were placed on the number of persons allowed to enter, qualitative controls were enacted to keep out the very poor, feebleminded, seriously ill, and "morally undesirable." In 1917 a literacy test was added to the physical, mental, and moral requirements. But with fewer than 75 mounted men assigned to patrol the 1,500-mile border, restrictions were difficult to enforce. Many Mexicans crossed into the United States without passing through a border station or paying the required head tax. These acts of illegal entry were encouraged by southwestern employers, who purposely voted against providing funds for better patrols and other enforcement measures. In this way, they made sure that the rapidly expanding farms and industries would not suffer a labor shortage. These nonenforcement policies, despite official regulations, made the border restrictions a legal fiction. Over half of the Mexican nationals who entered the United States before 1924 were able to avoid the legal formalities.

Crossing the border at El Paso, Texas. For many years, American officials made no attempt to patrol the border or to control migrations from Mexico.

Once in the Southwest, the newcomers often experienced feelings of disappointment and dismay. Having listened to the labor recruiters' promises about life in the United States, the workers came with great hopes and expectations that were soon shattered. Though used to extreme economic and social abuse, they were not prepared for the lack of personal interest shown by their American employers. The Mexican workers missed the attention that had traditionally been given them by their local bosses. In the United States they were often treated like cattle. They experienced unfair hiring and firing practices, unsanitary living conditions, and prejudices regarding their race and religion. Recruited for certain jobs, they were sometimes abandoned when no longer needed. In 1921, for example, 10,000 Mexican workers were stranded in Arizona after the cotton boom of the First World War exploded. Unable to pay for travel, these workers were left penniless during the entire winter season.

Despite the inhumane treatment that they often received in the United States, most of the Mexicans stayed, knowing that the chances of earning at least some wages were greater north of the border. For the number who returned, disillusioned, to Mexico, there were replacements who entered the United States, seeking opportunities. Each year more Mexicans moved north, and each year more remained. Since each Mexican child born in the United States was automatically a citizen, regardless of his parents' legal status or citizenship, the number of Mexican-Americans quickly exceeded the number of alien Mexicans.

The peak year of Mexican immigration was 1924, when over 89,000 persons entered the United States from Mexico on permanent visas. In the same year, a law was passed which assigned immigration quotas to the European countries, limiting the number of immigrants allowed to enter from each country. Quotas were not assigned to Mexico or to any country in the Western Hemisphere; this policy reflected the United States' concern about her diplomatic relationships with her neighbors. But immigration from Mexico was, nevertheless, affected by the 1924 Immigration Act. The reduction of European immigration caused the Mexican portion of total immigrations to expand and appear out of hand to many Americans. Congress began to debate the desirability of numerical restrictions on immigrations from Mexico. At this time, passage across the border was made more difficult. Arrangements to enter the United States could no longer be made at border stations. Mexicans wishing to emigrate had to file their applications, get a Mexican passport, and also obtain an American visa. Each step required a payment and this, plus the cost of travel, made the price of legal admission unusually expensive.

Though a Border Patrol was organized in 1924 to prevent illegal immigration from Mexico, those wishing to avoid the various fees devised ways to cross the border undetected. Both the employers and the prospective employees sought to avoid the difficulties of legal immigration. Law enforcement officials at the border cooperated by looking the other way when more labor was needed. Employers hired professional smugglers, sometimes called "coyotes," to bring in illegal immigrants. The labor smugglers helped the Mexicans to enter the United States by various means, including crossing the border concealed in automobiles, carts, or trucks and wading across the Rio Grande at night. Often forged passports and head-tax receipts were provided. Once across the line, the coyote turned the Mexican worker over to an *enganchista*, or labor contractor, who sold him, for a fee, to some agriculture, railroad, or mining employer. The coyote and the *enganchista* each made a handsome profit for bringing in the "wetbacks," as the illegal immigrants were called.

The employers also profited by the arrangement. They obtained a highly flexible work force of laborers who would work for wages below those accepted by others. Having no legal rights, the wetbacks were prevented from protesting about working conditions. They were unable to strike. Moreover, they themselves could be employed as strikebreakers. (Because many Mexican workers could not speak or understand English, they were often unaware that they were being used to break strikes.) The wetbacks were taken advantage of in other ways. On occasion agricultural employers hired the illegal aliens and reported them to immigration officials, but only after the season's work was done and before the wages were paid.

By 1929, close to 500,000 Mexicans had entered the United States on permanent visas. At least as many were in the country either illegally or on temporary visas, causing the total number of Mexican-born persons in the United States to reach at least 1 million. The newcomers aroused many different reactions among native Americans who lived in the Southwest. Employers

Illegal immigrants from Mexico were sometimes smuggled across the border hidden in automobiles or trucks.

viewed them as an economic asset, appreciating the low cost and availability of their labor. Social service workers and sociologists found the Mexican immigrants an interesting group to study. They subjected the Mexican population to numerous surveys, investigations, and clinical conferences. Other Americans saw the Mexicans only as an "alien" and largely unassimilated people. They were viewed in a variety of other ways, but they were seldom seen or treated as individuals.

Reactions varied in the Mexican-American communities, too. Hispanic people in New Mexico rarely associated with the newcomers. Having little contact with modern Mexico or the industrial world, the sheepherders of Spanish descent, for instance, considered themselves quite a different people. The proud descendants of early California settlers reacted like the Hispanic New Mexicans, resenting any association with those who came from modern Mexico. Members of the Mexican-American middle and upper classes also cared little for the majority of newcomers, viewing them with the same patronizing attitude with which they had always viewed the Mexican peons. Other Mexican-Americans felt threatened by the influx of cheap labor that competed for their jobs. Some, however, welcomed the Mexican immigrants as relatives and countrymen.

Only after the 1924 precedent of restrictions was established did Anglo-Americans outside the Southwest become involved with the "problem" of Mexicans. The question of assigning a quota to Mexico, similar to the quotas for European countries, caused much controversy in Congress, with testimony and arguments put forth on both sides of the issue. Major Southwest employers objected to numerical restrictions because they considered an inexpensive labor force a necessity. Many statesmen were also opposed to a quota. They were concerned about the United States' relationship with her neighbors, fearing the repercussions that could result from singling out Mexico for a quota. Joining the antirestrictionists were those who still believed that the United States should not abandon its ideal of being a "melting pot" where immigrants from all countries could become part of the American population.

Because agricultural employers in the Southwest depended on the cheap labor provided by Mexican workers, they resisted efforts to restrict immigration from Mexico.

Arguing on the other side of the issue, the advocates of a strict restriction policy stressed economic and racial considerations. American labor unions expressed the viewpoint that Mexicans hindered the progress of American workers by working for less money and thus driving down the wage scale. Eastern and midwestern businessmen wanted restrictions that would prevent Southwestern employers from taking advantage of this "alien" resource. Eugenicists (people who want to improve the genetic character of the human race) and members of patriotic societies were worried about the composition of the American population. Labeling the Mexicans "racially inferior" because of their Indian heritage, spokesmen from these groups warned against permitting such a "mongrel" population to mix with "American blood."

After a five-year debate over the issue of Mexican immigration, the federal government finally took action in January 1929. It solved the problem very neatly, satisfying the restrictionists without actually passing a law that would be offensive to the Mexican government. By enforcing three existing rulings, administrative controls were made to take on a "squeeze effect" which restricted immigrations. Strict enforcement of the literacy test authorized in 1917 resulted in the rejection of many uneducated laborers. The other two rules, used in combination, were the Contract Labor Law of 1885 and the clause of the 1924 immigration law which states that persons "likely to become a public charge" could be refused entry. When applying for a visa, the Mexican worker was asked if he had a job waiting in the United States. A "yes" answer could disqualify him on the basis of the Contract Labor Law, which forbids foreign recruitment of labor. His alternative, a "no" answer, could disqualify him as a person "likely to become a public charge." In this way, legal immigration from Mexico was nearly halted in 1929.

In Texas, another restrictive measure, the Texas Emigrant Agent Law, also took effect in 1929. This law grew out of the Texas cotton growers' fear that they were losing their valuable labor supply to the sugar beet growers from other states who recruited in Texas and then kept the workers throughout the year. Attempting to teach the sugar beet agents a lesson, the Texas growers shot holes in the tires of their trucks and prevented Mexicans, by force, from meeting with the agents. When the Texas Emigrant Agent Law made out-of-state recruitment illegal, labor smugglers diversified their activities. They smuggled Mexican labor not only over the international border but also over state borders. At times a coyote would deliver laborers to a Texas grower, then later steal them and deliver them to a different employer, collecting a fee each time. To prevent this from happening, the employers guarded their Mexican workers and sometimes even gagged and tied them.

Shortly after the passage of immigration restrictions, the effects of the Great Depression began to be felt in the United States. The flow of immigration that had nearly been halted in 1929 turned and flowed toward Mexico in the 1930s. Because the Mexican laborers were viewed only as a convenience, they were subject to the needs and whims of the American majority. The same labor force that had been eagerly sought in the 1920s was rejected in the 1930s when the economic hardships in the Southwest were complicated by natural disasters. Soil erosion destroyed Oklahoma farms, while Texas cotton became so unprofitable that vast areas of the Texas Panhandle and west

Texas turned from cotton back to cattle. As a result of these conditions, Mexican laborers found themselves unneeded. Agriculture, particularly in California, replaced Mexican workers with workers fleeing the Dust Bowl and urban workers escaping city poverty. Unable to find work, many Mexican-Americans were forced to apply for welfare in order to support their families.

Anglo-Americans resented the idea that "unassimilated aliens" were applying for welfare. To make matters worse, employers felt no responsibility for the workers they had recruited less than 10 years before. Therefore, measures were taken to reduce the number of Mexicans in the United States. Immigration Service officers stepped up the search and deportation procedures for illegal aliens. At the same time, local welfare agencies began to make plans for "repatriating" Mexicans, thereby ridding their overloaded welfare lists of this burden.

The idea of "repatriation" came from many sources. Mexico had started a repatriation program a few years earlier in an attempt to win back some of the emigrants who had left the country during the civil war. (About 10 percent of the population had emigrated during these years.) Influential Mexicans and Mexican-Americans took a cue from this program, suggesting and encouraging voluntary repatriation from the United States. In a study published in 1930, Manuel Gamio, an American sociologist of Mexican birth, observed that Mexicans had failed to assimilate into American society. Therefore, he concluded, repatriation would be best for everyone. Sharing this view, Diego Rivera, a Mexican artist residing in Detroit at the time, proposed the idea of repatriating Mexican laborers to the city council.

Considering federal action toward repatriation too slow and cautious, local agencies devised a workable scheme for sending the Mexicans "home." They arranged for special railroad cars to transport people willing to return to Mexico. In an economically brilliant plan, the agencies paid the fare to the border; the cost of transportation per person was less than the cost of one week's board and lodging. By such methods of mass repatriation, nearly 89,000 Mexican aliens departed in the 1930s, along with many others having Spanish surnames.

Mexicans waiting to board special trains that will take them back to Mexico, 1931. Their "repatriation" is being paid for by the Los Angeles County Charities Department.

Though some legal residents voluntarily packed up their belongings and returned to Mexico by car or train, most were coerced into "volunteering" for repatriation. Various means were used to encourage the "volunteers." Most commonly, welfare payments were stopped unless the person agreed to be deported. In many cities of the West and Midwest, Mexicans who applied for relief were referred to variously named "Mexican bureaus." At the bureau, officials talked with heads of Mexican families, attempting to obtain a declaration of their desire to return to Mexico. In addition to the Mexican aliens, naturalized citizens and American-born citizens of Mexican ancestry were frequently referred to the bureaus, where protests that they did not desire repatriation were ignored and rights of citizenship were denied.

For years Mexicans in America had been discussing "going home" to Mexico someday. Few, however, seriously planned the trip. Forced to return by repatriations, these Americanized Mexicans discovered that they no longer fit into Mexican life.

Though many were welcomed into their native villages, conflicts ensued. They were called "gringos" because of their American ways and were accused of being pagans, destroyers of old customs, and freakish intruders.

Mexican-Americans who were repatriated to Mexico during the 1930s found Mexican village life very different from life in the United States.

The Mexicans and Mexican-Americans had great difficulty in adjusting to village life in Mexico. Parents and young children had the fewest adjustment problems: the men, often used to migrating, had had little time to get used to a particular spot; mothers were often more concerned with their families than with the location; and young children had not yet become Americanized. The older children, however, were caught between the two cultures. They had "American" friends, "American" ways, and often spoke both Spanish and English or a combination of the two. Though opportunities in the United States were limited, they did not feel at home in the Mexican villages and wished to return across the border. Most of the native-born Americans, constituting more than half of those repatriated, shared this view. When these youngsters later wished to reenter the United States, however, they were told that they could lose their citizenship and be excluded if they had served in the Mexican army or voted in Mexican elections. This possibility had never been mentioned to those who "volunteered for repatriation."

PART III

A Community Emerges

1. *Feeling Permanent*

After the repatriations of the depression years, people of Mexican ancestry who continued to live in the United States developed a new perspective on their place in American life. There were only 377,000 Mexican-born people in the United States in 1940, compared with 639,000 in 1930, but those who remained considered themselves Mexican-Americans. The Anglo-Americans, too, began to take a new look at the Mexican communities, for the first time regarding them as permanent parts of American society.

With this new outlook, both Anglos and Mexican-Americans began to examine the situation of the Mexican-American in the United States. Both groups gained a new awareness of the discrimination patterns that had developed over the last hundred years. Some states permitted discrimination in such places as lunch counters, bars, cafes, drive-ins, hotels, and recreation centers. In some areas movies, schools, churches, and cemeteries were also segregated. Separate times had been set up for Mexicans to use department stores and recreation areas.

A street in the Mexican barrio of Los Angeles

The isolation of the Mexican-Americans from the rest of American society could be seen most clearly in the *barrios*, the urban neighborhoods which were home to many Mexicans and other Spanish-speaking people. The barrio of Los Angeles was the largest in the United States, and it was the scene for the most significant activities of Mexican-Americans in the 1940s.

Youngsters of the Los Angeles barrio led troubled lives during the years of the Second World War. Caught between two cultures, they fit into neither. Their language, values, and mannerisms were more Americanized than those of their parents. Yet the Anglo-American community discriminated against them for being too "Mexican." Not comfortable in either of the two cultures, many of these young people joined together in neighborhood street gangs.

In an effort to break up the gangs, city police frequently picked up and arrested members for attacks on rival gangs. The newspapers published sensationalized stories of each gang conflict, and as a result of this publicity, public pressure rose in the city, calling for an end to the boys' gangs. On August 2, 1942, the opportunity presented itself for the police to "clean up" the latest "Mexican problem." After finding the body of José Diaz near the Sleepy Lagoon swimming hole, the Los Angeles Police Department proceeded to arrest 300 Mexican-American teenagers. Twenty-two members of the 38th Street gang were placed on trial for the murder of Diaz, even though there were no witnesses to the alleged crime. Nine of the teenagers were convicted of second-degree murder and assault, while three were convicted of first-degree murder. The 12 were sentenced to San Quentin prison.

On the day of the mass arrests a grand jury investigation was begun, and a Special Mexican Relations Committee was appointed to hold public hearings on the problems of Mexican youths. The hearings disclosed some of the attitudes which the Los Angeles police had toward Mexican-Americans. A police lieutenant explaining the "reasons" for the gang crimes declared that though they were partly due to the economic conditions of the home and the lack of recreational facilities, the main cause was race. "Crime is a matter of race," he contended, and the tendency to commit crimes can be inherited. For this reason he felt that the "race must be punished." The hearing had uncovered some of the real causes of barrio problems. There was little

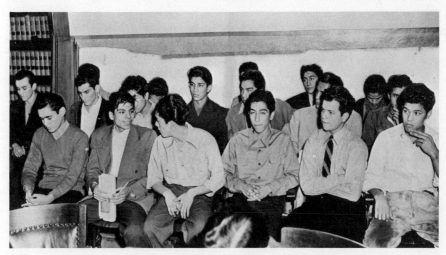

The defendants in the Sleepy Lagoon case

question that the police had taken special pains to harass and arrest members of the East Los Angeles barrio.

It was not surprising that many people saw the trial and conviction of the Sleepy Lagoon defendants as a conspiracy against all Mexican-Americans. After the conviction of the 12 boys, a Sleepy Lagoon Defense Committee was formed to work for an appeal of the court's decision. But the committee itself soon became the subject of another investigation. The Tenney Commission, a special committee of the California legislature whose purpose was to investigate un-American activities in the state, questioned the organization and purpose of the Sleepy Lagoon Defense Committee. Its findings reported that the Defense Committee was a "typical communist front organization." Despite this condemnation, the committee succeeded in its national campaign for funds to appeal the court decision. In October 1944, the district court of appeals reversed the verdict that had convicted the boys of murder. For the first time, Mexican-Americans won an organized victory in the courts.

The Sleepy Lagoon case was only one of the conflicts in wartime Los Angeles between the barrios and the Anglo community. During the winter of 1942-43, a race riot exploded in the city. These so-called zoot-suit attacks were set off by a number of factors—war tensions, the Tenney Commission operations, and the number of military men in the coastal city looking for a last fling.

Zoot suits were outfits worn by barrio youths to symbolize their rebellion against the bonds of many traditions. The boys donned long suit coats and trousers that pegged at the cuffs, draped around the knee, and had deep pleats at the waist. This costume was worn with a low-hanging watch chain. Girls of the barrios also had a new look—short skirts, net stockings, extra-high-heeled shoes, and elaborate hairdos. The zoot-suit garb, meaningful to young people of the barrios, took on a different meaning to the outside community. Because newspapers were forbidden to use the term *Mexican* in a derogatory way, they substituted the term *zoot-suiters*. In this way, the newspapers made "zoot-suit" seem to be synonymous with "delinquent conduct."

During the years of the zoot-suit craze, soldiers and sailors in Los Angeles often sought out the companionship of the barrio girls, and the young men of the barrio frequently conflicted with these uniformed invaders of their territory. One night, 11 sailors reported that they had been attacked by a large number of Mexican-American boys. The following night, 200 sailors cruised through the Mexican section of the city in taxis, beating up all youths wearing zoot-suits. Newspapers played up the event in a sensational story. The next night, soldiers and marines joined the sailors and again the newspapers reported the story in a sensational manner. Following the newspaper report of a riot, a mob of several thousand civilians and military personnel beat up zoot-suiters and other youths of Mexican appearance. Streetcars were halted while minority youths were pulled out of their seats and horribly beaten. Zoot-suits were ripped off the victims, who were then left bleeding and naked on the streets. As a result of these brutal events, the *victims* of the assaults were arrested, and it became a misdemeanor to wear a zoot-suit.

A mob of servicemen stop a streetcar on a Los Angeles street during the zoot-suit riots of 1943.

Sergeants **Macario Garcia** (left) and **Cleto Rodriquez** (right) were among the 17 Mexican-Americans awarded the Congressional Medal of Honor during World War II.

But while chaos prevailed on the home front in Los Angeles, Mexican-American soldiers were experiencing a different awareness of being an "American." Most of the approximately 300,000 Mexican-American men who served in the armed forces during World War II had their first opportunity to see the world outside of their home community. Brought together by the wartime army, they were able to compare experiences and share the novelty of living in a place where they were not considered inferior.

The Mexican-American soldiers accumulated many honors for their military service. Seventeen were awarded the Congressional Medal of Honor. Two units made up of Mexican-Americans from New Mexico, Texas, and Arizona played an important role at the Battle of Bataan. An all-Chicano infantry company—Company E, 141st Regiment of the 36th Division—was one of the most decorated of World War II. Marines, paratroopers, tank corpsmen, and those who served in other branches of the service also earned respect for their bravery and their outstanding efforts.

A new kind of Mexican-American community emerged after World War II. When the soldiers returned home, they met those who had recently experienced the open hostilities in Los Angeles.

They also came in contact with people who had recently returned from Mexico, having realized how Americanized they had become. The soldiers themselves had a new feeling of unity with members of the Mexican-American community who lived in different parts of the country. They also had a new desire to be accepted by the country for which they had fought so bravely and for which their friends had died.

In the past, most Mexicanos had tried to cope with the society that considered them "the Mexican problem" rather than to change it. Self-reliance groups had been formed to protect their members from the necessity of dealing with the larger community. *Mutualistas*, or mutual-benefit societies, provided funeral and death benefits, financial aid, insurance against accidents or sickness, and other necessities. The *Alianza Hispano Americano*, formed in 1894, was one of the largest groups of this kind.

Disassociation from the Mexican-American community was another method used to avoid being involved in the "Mexican problem." Following this tactic, many Mexican-Americans had left the barrios at their first opportunity. An alternative was to assume a group name other than "Mexican," because most prejudices were connected with that name. The names "Spanish," "Hispanic," and "Latin" were preferable.

After World War II, however, the idea of combating problems instead of adapting to them gained popularity. The first steps were taken by the veterans, who used their G.I. benefits to gain personal advancement. Because of the G.I. Bill they were able to finance educations in colleges, and trade and technical schools. Some bought homes and started businesses. Those who had been civilians utilized the new skills gained in war-related industries to advance in their occupations. With new pride in *La Raza*—the people—the postwar Mexican-Americans attempted to improve the barrios as they improved themselves.

Various methods were used by those who wanted to help the community. Some joined the League of United Latin American Citizens (LULAC) and other groups dedicated to assimilation into Anglo-American society. These groups attempted to "Americanize" the Mexican-Americans, while seeking to preserve the

Mexican culture. They encouraged patriotism and learning of the English language. Others tried political means, considering political power the key to opening new opportunities. The arena of educational problems was the main target of reform for some. Courtrooms also provided the setting for battles against discrimination. Labor problems, too, were attacked in an attempt to deal with the central problem of poverty. Though all these problems were familiar to both the Mexican-American and Anglo-American communities, the experiences of World War II caused many to seek new solutions with a new sense of urgency.

2. Postwar Progress: Political Means

In the years that followed World War II many groups were formed to increase the political power of Mexican-Americans. They all sought to gain recognition for their people, to obtain representation, and to bring about meaningful changes in attitudes and policies. But they varied in their methods. The earlier groups concentrated on nonpartisan, community-level politics. Later groups were involved with partisan politics. They were followed by organizations that advocated Chicano party politics.

The grass-roots organizations were community-based efforts formed to increase voter registration and to promote Mexican-Americans in local elections. The three main groups responsible for directing political attention to the Mexican-Americans were the Unity Leagues, the Community Service Organization (CSO), and the G.I. Forum of Texas. Voter registration programs of the California-based CSO and Unity Leagues helped to get over 40,000 new voters registered in the California barrios. By supporting Mexican-Americans running in local elections, the Unity Leagues brought out enough votes to make officials aware of a new political power base. The G.I. Forum was instrumental in the fight to repeal the poll tax in Texas.

Besides their political activities, the groups also concerned themselves with social action. The G.I. Forum Veterans' group raised money for civil rights actions throughout the Southwest. The CSO started English language classes, helped people understand instructions and fill out income tax forms and social security

A voter registration drive conducted by the West
Los Angeles Community Service Organization.

applications, and set up Spanish language classes to help older
residents become citizens. In addition, the CSO was instrumental
in the passage of a law that made noncitizens eligible for old-age
assistance. Fighting for better law enforcement, they also gained
victories against the police in both the courts and the newspapers.

In 1953, the Council of Mexican American Affairs (CMAA)
was formed to coordinate the efforts of various groups concerned
with the betterment of the Mexican-American. This group,
which consisted of many business, professional, and labor leaders,
was interested primarily in changing the image of Mexican-
Americans from blue collar to white collar. CMAA emphasized
the idea that members of La Raza can make a unique contribution
to American society because they are a bilingual and bicultural
people (that is, they speak two languages and share in two different cultures). Though this centralizing organization was
short lived, it held many conferences on the plight of Mexican-
Americans and increased public concern about existing problems.

Groups formed in the 1960s were more involved with partisan politics. Of these, the Mexican American Political Association (MAPA) and the Political Association of Spanish Speaking Organizations (PASSO or PASO) were the largest and most influential. MAPA organized to take stands on political issues, present and endorse candidates for office, register voters, and carry on political education programs. In 1962, three of its endorsed candidates were elected to office. Edward Roybal was chosen to represent California in the United States House of Representatives; he was the first Mexican-American ever elected to the federal legislature. At the same time, Philip Soto and John Moreno were elected to the California legislature. In 1968 MAPA succeeded in achieving another first when Alex Garcia was elected to the California State Assembly.

Edward Roybal

Juan Cornejo

Though agreeing with the objectives of MAPA, many Spanish-speaking people in Texas objected to the name. Because they considered themselves Latin-Americans rather than Mexican-Americans, they formed the Political Association of Spanish Speaking Organizations. One of the most significant victories resulting from the work of PASSO was the 1963 election of Juan Cornejo as mayor of Crystal City, Texas. Though the population of Crystal City was largely Mexican-American, this was an unprecedented election upset for the Texas town. Together, PASSO and MAPA have succeeded in getting Mexican-Americans elected to local office in both Texas and California.

The new political involvement was a hopeful sign to many. These people saw the gains in political representation as significant, but others disagreed. To them, the gains appeared to be merely token accomplishments when compared to the existing problems. Inspired by the successes of black militants, they turned to militant tactics in order to gain rights. But at the same time that a militant Chicano movement was taking shape, the government was paying increased attention to the problems of Mexican-Americans. And as the government realized the need to identify and solve the problems of the barrios, Mexican-Americans demanded a larger role in government programs. Along with this quest for control, the Mexican-Americans gained a self-awareness and a new pride in their heritage.

The first major act of government recognition of Mexican-Americans as a group with real problems was the plan for a White House conference in 1965. Though greatly anticipated by Mexican-Americans, this event never occurred. Instead, a meeting with the federal Equal Employment Opportunities Commission was scheduled for March 1966. This Albuquerque meeting met with criticism, for, instead of a full White House conference, the Mexican-Americans were given the opportunity to speak to only one government representative. Fifty leaders of La Raza walked out of the meeting, complaining that the White House had displayed too little interest. The group demanded to be heard, forcing further government action. A few months after the Albuquerque Walkout, President Lyndon Johnson, responding to the pressure, met with five Mexican-American leaders. As a result of this meeting, a Cabinet Committee on Mexican American Affairs was formed. The first step had been taken toward finding a solution to the problems facing Mexican-Americans.

Another conference was set up in October 1967 to allow Mexican-Americans to describe their position and explain the problems as they saw them. Though this conference, held in El Paso, was an improvement over the meeting in Albuquerque, it too was heavily criticized. Both the poor and the young were excluded from representation at the meeting. With very little audience participation allowed and with the more radical leaders uninvited, the El Paso conference seemed to lack meaning. Many speakers testified, but the conference was rejected by community leaders, who organized their own conference to run in El Paso.

At the rival La Raza Unida Conference held in El Paso in 1967, a new type of Chicano movement was started. Those who no longer accepted the government's method of problem solving formed their own groups to force action that would benefit their people. Both the young and the poor were welcomed and encouraged to become involved. Most of the new leaders were present at the La Raza Unida Conference, which was presided over by Ernesto Galarza. Bert Corona, president of MAPA, was there, along with Rudolfo "Corky" Gonzales of *La Crusada Para la Justicia* (the Crusade for Justice), Reies Tijerina of the *Alianza Federal de los Pueblos Libres* (Federal Alliance of Free City States), and José Gutierrez, founder of MAYO, the Mexican American Youth Organization. From this conference came a new spirit of revolution and a newly accepted name: the young activists called themselves *Chicanos*. The word was originally a slang shortening of "Mexican," but it became a symbol of pride and solidarity to many.

After the El Paso conference, the more militant leaders started Chicano movements that promoted a feeling of Chicano nationalism. "Corky" Gonzales of Denver, Colorado, urged the formation of a National Chicano Party and started Chicano Youth Liberation conferences. José Gutierrez established the La Raza Unida Party as an independent political party. Gradually, Chicano politics spread throughout the country, appealing to the young and the more radical. This new political movement received both acclaim as the liberation of Chicanos and criticism for being a "politics of race."

Another offshoot of the La Raza Unida conference in El Paso was the formation of the Southwest Council of La Raza. Former

José Gutierrez (left) and **Rudolfo "Corky" Gonzales** at the national convention of the La Raza Unida Party in 1972. Gutierrez established the party after the El Paso conference of Chicano leaders held in 1967.

CSO leader Herman Gallegos became the executive director of this group. Funded by the Ford Foundation, the council provides assistance to grass-roots groups wishing to become more effectively involved in civic affairs. It also promotes research and publications directed toward helping the Mexican-American.

The work of an organization such as the Southwest Council of La Raza has contributed much toward the goal of increased political opportunities for Mexican-Americans. In recent years, the federal government has also continued to recognize the needs and demands of the Mexican-American community. Starting with the cabinet-level committee named by President Johnson in 1967, the government has attempted to focus its efforts on problems of the Mexican-Americans. When the cabinet committee became the Inter-Agency on Mexican American Affairs, its chairman, Vicente T. Ximenes, became the chairman of the new organization. Ximenes later became the first Mexican-American member of the Equal Employment Opportunity Commission and vice-president of the National Urban Coalition.

In December 1969, the Inter-Agency on Mexican American Affairs was reorganized again and renamed the Cabinet Committee on Opportunity for the Spanish Speaking. Martin Castello, the last chairman of the inter-agency, continued as chairman of the new committee. Its objective has been to make sure that federal programs were reaching all Mexican-Americans and other Spanish-speaking people and providing the assistance they need. The Committee on Opportunity has the authority to establish any new programs that may be necessary to handle the problems unique to Spanish-speaking people in the United States.

In the late 1960s, Spanish surnames also began to appear in other government positions. Hilary Sandoval became the administrator of the Small Business Administration (SBA) in March 1969. As the head of the SBA, Sandoval could assist Mexican-Americans in the fields of industry, commerce, and finance. Another appointment, in 1969, made Tony Rodriguez chairman of the United States section of the United States-Mexican Joint Border Commission. A new commissioner of the Civil Rights Commission, Manuel Ruiz, Jr., took office in January 1970, when Hector P. Garcia, founder of the G.I. Forum and commissioner since 1968, stepped down.

In 1971 even more Mexican-Americans came to hold federal government positions. Philip Sanchez became the head of the Office of Economic Opportunity (OEO) in May of that year. At the same time, Philip Montez attained the position of director of the Western Field Office of the United States Commission on Civil Rights. Lorenzo Ramirez was put in charge of the Southwest Field Office of the Community Relations Service. Men of Mexican descent were also appointed directors of two field offices of the Department of Housing and Urban Development: Raymond Carrasco became head of the Los Angeles area office and Manuel Sanchez of the Dallas office.

In the Office of Education, both Armando Rodriguez and Gilbert Chavez have held the position of director of the Office for Spanish-Speaking American Affairs.

Vicente T. Ximines

Manuel Ruiz, Jr.

Philip Sanchez

Romana Banuelos

Also in 1971, Romana Banuelos became the Treasurer of the United States. Though accused of employing illegal Mexican immigrants in her Texas industry, Mrs. Banuelos was confirmed for the important government position. With this appointment she became the highest ranking Mexican-American in government office.

3. *Postwar Progress: Civil Rights*

Since the Treaty of Guadalupe-Hidalgo, when the Southwest became part of the United States, all Mexican-Americans have been guaranteed the civil rights that belong to other American citizens. But the most basic of these rights, the right to fair and equal treatment, has often been denied. Over the years inequities have been uncovered in the areas of education, police treatment, property rights, and due process of law.

Possibly the most important inequity is in the field of education: though Mexican-American children have the legal right to an equal education, common practice has often kept them from receiving one. Many children of Mexican descent were discouraged from attending schools, both by school administrators and by the poor farmworkers who needed their children's help in the fields to support the family. In many cases the compulsory education laws were completely ignored.

For the children who did attend school, educational problems still existed. Because of their Mexican heritage, students often attended inferior schools, isolated from the Anglo-American population and staffed by teachers who were seldom qualified. The schools taught cultural values that differed from those the children learned at home. They attempted to eliminate the "Mexican traits" and cultural heritage, punishing those who spoke Spanish, even though it was their native language and the one used at home. (For many years California and Texas had laws which made it illegal to use Spanish in and around schools.) Frequently Mexican-American children were labeled "retarded" on the basis of culturally biased I.Q. tests that were written in English.

The first organized protest against these practices occurred in 1930, when a Texas family filed suit in a federal court, charging that separate schools denied their children equal protection under the law. They failed to win the case, however, and the court ruled that segregation of schools was legal in Texas. But this case, despite its result, did start a new trend. Other Mexican-Americans began arguing their cases in court, and schools were pressured into enacting voluntary reforms.

After World War II, the fight for better education gained momentum. With more Mexican-Americans living in urban areas, education became more important, and a new look was taken at the quality of education available. In 1946 Mexican-Americans succeeded for the first time in a legal action against the schools. In that year, Gonzalo Mendez filed suit in federal court, charging

Young Mexican-Americans have often found it difficult to get a good education in the United States.

that the school districts of southern California discriminated illegally against children of Mexican descent by maintaining separate facilities for them. The court ruled in favor of the children and asked the schools not to segregate. The decision in the case of *Mendez* v. *the Westminster School District et al.* laid the groundwork for desegregation cases of the 1950s.

Soon after the California case, a suit was filed to end segregation in Texas. The 1948 case of *Delgado* v. *the Bastrop Independent School District* resulted in a ruling that segregation of Mexican-American children was illegal. The rulings in the California and Texas cases both ended the legal support for deliberately maintained segregation. Though segregated schools continued to exist, the first major round in the battle against discrimination had been won.

Interest in education increased in the years that followed. Veterans who had used the G.I. Bill to gain an education showed great concern about the education of their children. During the 1950s and early sixties, marked increases could be seen in the amount of schooling attained by Mexican-Americans; more people went to school, and those who went stayed longer. New programs were also initiated to improve the education that Mexican-Americans received. In 1956 the Texas-based League of United Latin American Citizens started the Little School of the 400. This preschool program attempted to teach basic English to children from non-English-speaking homes. The program met with success: at least 95 percent of the participants entered school at the same level as the English-speaking children and continued without being held back because of a deficiency in English. The success of the Little School of the 400 encouraged the Texas legislature to fund a similar program for the entire school district and later led to the federally funded Operation Headstart program for preschool youngsters.

By 1968, Mexican-Americans were no longer content to accept minor improvements. They felt they were being cheated by the education system, and they demanded fast and drastic changes. In response, Congress passed the Bilingual Education Act, initiating the first educational reform with a national scope. Funds were provided for programs that involve the use of two languages, one of which is English, as a medium of instruction. Also, provisions were made for the study of the history and culture associated with the non-English language. Since 90 percent of such programs involve Spanish as one of the languages, this act constituted a major effort to attack the worst problem faced by Mexican-American school children—the language difficulty. Soon other programs followed, allowing English to

Bilingual education programs have made it possible for Mexican-American children to use their native language in the classroom.

be taught as a second language and enabling students to take advantage of their bicultural heritage.

A 1968 suit filed by 32 Mexican-American families for their children also caused major changes in the pace of reform. The case of *Cisneros* v. *Corpus Christi Independent School District* resulted in a 1970 decision that the school district was operating a segregated school system and thus discriminating against Mexican-American children. The United States District Court judge ordered the district to submit a desegregation plan. This breakthrough was followed by other cases won in favor of the Mexican-Americans. In May 1970, a U.S. district court ordered 17 Denver schools to desegregate and to improve the quality of education. Most of the schools had predominantly Mexican-American students. Then, in August 1970, the Justice Department brought the state of Texas and 26 of its school districts to court for having resisted voluntary desegregation arrangements. The schools were charged with discrimination against Mexican-Americans as well as Negroes.

Though these cases appeared to be a hopeful sign of progress, events in 1971 showed that the courtroom battle against segregation of schools was still far from won. In that year a district court ruled that the government failed to prove that the Austin, Texas, school district discriminated against Mexican-Americans. The advances made by the 1970 Corpus Christi case were also halted when school officials in that city were granted a delay in putting into effect a desegregation plan that called for busing. The court ruled that it was questionable whether Corpus Christi had deliberately segregated Mexican-Americans.

The Mexican-Americans' fight for improved education has taken place not only in courtrooms but also in the schools themselves. In 1968, Los Angeles was the scene of a militant student strike known as the "blowout," which brought Mexican-American students into the struggle. Rebelling against the city's education system, more than 15,000 Chicano high school students walked out of East Los Angeles high schools. Thirteen were arrested and charged with conspiracy to cause the walkout—an offense considered a felony. One of the 13 was a teacher who was also

Teachers and students protest the arrest of Mexican-Americans taking part in the student strike in East Los Angeles high schools, 1968.

suspended from his teaching duties. To protest the arrests and suspensions, students held a sit-in at the Los Angeles Board of Education.

Walkouts throughout the Southwest followed the Los Angeles activities. By the end of spring 1968, the students had succeeded in forcing the board to reinstate the teacher and to hear their demands. Leaders of the "blowout" asked for reforms that dealt with both general and specific educational problems. Among the specific requests were: smaller classes, classes about their heritage, and classes with vocational relevance. To continue the fight for these reforms, the Educational Issues Coordinating Committee (EICC) organized and waged a campaign of publicity and action.

Other student groups also organized to fight for educational reform. Best known of the high school and college-level Chicano groups are the United Mexican American Students (UMAS), the Mexican American Student Organization (MASO), the Mexican American Youth Organization (MAYO), the Mexican American Student Confederation (MASC), and the National Organization of Mexican American Students (NOMAS). These groups have been active in pressing for Chicano studies programs in individual high schools and colleges and for the admission of more Chicanos to colleges. Recently, many of these groups have become part of MECHA—*Movimento Estudiantil Chicano de Aztlán*.

The federal Migrant Children Educational Assistance Act of 1960 started educational improvements in a different area. Children of migrant workers have historically received a poor education because their families move frequently while following the crops. Forced to miss school and attend several schools during the year, most of the children are years behind in their education, and few ever finish high school. Recently, the public has become aware of these problems, and summer school programs are currently offered to help these children get an education. New programs have also been initiated to have school records sent to each of the schools attended. These programs are designed to enable students to receive a continuous education, despite the necessity of attending many schools.

The changes of the past few decades have focused national attention on educational problems, but the problems are still far from being solved. Migrant children are still behind in schools; schools are still segregated; and few Mexican-Americans ever graduate from high school. Today the average educational level of Mexican-Americans is 8.3 years, as compared with the average of 11.2 years for Anglo-Americans. Over 42 percent drop out of school before high school graduation. Of the entire Mexican-American population, 28 percent have severe reading problems, as compared with 4 percent of Anglo-Americans. Mexican-American students are still having difficulty grasping subjects taught in English while they are just learning the language. More than half of the students attend schools that are predominantly Mexican-American, often staffed with inferior teachers. In the

Lower Rio Grande Valley, for example, only 57 percent of the teachers have teaching credentials, and only 10 percent have a Bachelor of Arts degree. In addition, many teachers of Mexican-American children still think that "culturally different" means "culturally deprived" or "culturally inferior."

It is in the field of education that problems and denials of civil rights can be most easily seen. Civil rights, however, have also been violated in other areas. As recently as 1954, persons of Mexican descent were barred from jury duty. It took a Supreme Court ruling in May 1954 to put an end to the practice. This decision also caused the judges to set aside murder charges in the case of Pete Hernandez because no Mexican-Americans were on his jury panels.

Recently, the issue of police brutality has created much concern in the Mexican-American community. Two demonstrations have been held in an effort to bring about change. In 1971, 3,000 Mexican-Americans rioted in Los Angeles, protesting the police brutality that had allegedly occurred since August 1970. (It was in August that a Mexican-American newspaper columnist, Ruben Salazar, was killed by a police tear gas projectile.) In the violence of the Los Angeles riot, 1 man was killed and 50 injured during a battle with Los Angeles County sheriff's deputies.

The other 1971 demonstration was more peaceful. Hundreds of Mexican-Americans started on a march through small Texas towns in the Rio Grande Valley. By the time they had reached their destination, more than 2,000 demonstrators had gathered to protest police brutality. The demonstration ended after a memorial service was held for the five men and boys who had been killed by police during and after civil rights demonstrations in the valley since the summer of 1970.

One of the best known militant groups formed to fight for civil rights is the Brown Beret, started by David Sanchez in 1968. Modeled after the Black Panther Party, this organization was created as a self-defense measure against police brutality in the barrios. With the motto of "Serve-Observe-Protect," the young Chicanos maintain a form of law and order by patrolling the barrios of the Southwest.

Members of the Brown Beret have dedicated themselves
to the defense of the Chicano community.

An older group shares the militant spotlight but aims at a different aspect of civil rights. The *Alianza Federal de Mercedes* (Federal Alliance of Land Grants) was formed in 1963 to regain land once owned by holders of Spanish and Mexican land grants. According to Reies Lopez Tijerina, the organization's founder, the old land grants should have been protected by the Treaty of Guadalupe-Hidalgo. He claims that the treaty has been violated and questions the legality of the means by which grantees were separated from the land. In an effort to recapture the territory that they claim, Tijerina and members of the Alianza (called Aliancistas) have staged two rebellions. The first was an October 1966 attempt to take over the Kit Carson National Forest in northern New Mexico. Rebels "arrested" U.S. Forest Rangers for trespassing and took over government vehicles. Tijerina and members of the Alianza, however, were soon arrested for offenses related to the revolt.

On June 5, 1967, Tijerina and the organization, now called the *Alianza Federal de los Pueblos Libres*, were in the news again. This time, they proclaimed the existence of the Republic of Rio

Reies Tijerina addresses a group taking part in the Poor People's Campaign, 1968. Tijerina has been an active leader in the Chicanos' struggle for civil rights.

Chama in Rio Arriba County, New Mexico, and they attacked the Rio Arriba County Courthouse, freeing Aliancistas who had been jailed two days earlier because of their demands for federally held land-grant territory. Though the June 5 insurrection resulted in arrests, it brought to light the condition of poverty in New Mexico's Spanish-American population.

4. *Postwar Progress: Attack on Poverty*

Though not all Mexican-Americans have economic problems, poverty has been a historic dilemma for most. It has been more difficult for them to break out of the poverty mold than for immigrants from other countries. Because Mexico is a neighbor of the United States, most employers assumed that the Spanish-speaking people were only working north of the border temporarily. Reasoning that they could go "back home" if they didn't care for the United States, few Anglo-Americans were concerned about their plight. People who looked Mexican were rarely able to own land and seldom received the benefits of an education. Without land, education, or enough money to last the year without some form of credit, the wage laborers of the Southwest and the migrant labor routes became locked in a cycle of poverty.

As more Mexicans moved north, they joined the poverty cycle and perpetuated it. Though they were welcomed by native-born Mexican-Americans because they were part of La Raza, these newcomers created tremendous problems. The ceaseless flow of new laborers from Mexico slowed progress in improving working conditions. Yet attempts were made to achieve progress. From time to time men and women revolted against the conditions which held their people down. One of the earliest acts of protest took place in 1883; led by Juan Gomez, hundreds of cowboys went on strike against cattlemen in the Texas Panhandle. In 1903, over 1,000 Mexican and Japanese beet workers struck in Ventura, California.

By 1927, Mexican workers had their first lasting agricultural unions. Largest of these unions was the *Confederación de Uniones Obreras Mexicanos* (CUOM), which, in 1928, demanded an improvement in the contract system of hiring, higher wages, and better working conditions in the fields. When the growers refused to negotiate, a strike was called in time for the cantaloupe harvest in the Imperial Valley. Two years later, another strike was called, but this time the growers settled. In 1933, two more farm strikes were called by Mexican workers, followed by another two strikes in Southern California in 1936.

These union strikes had many things in common. All were prompted by a meager annual family wage of not more than $600 per year, by poor housing, and by discrimination. And all were disrupted by violence and the deportation of leaders and strikers. Local Anglo communities were mainly interested in "protecting their farmers," by which they meant the farm owners, not the workers. But despite the overall failure of the strikes, they did produce some improved working conditions. State agencies and growers were shown the necessity for changing the contract system. As a result, contractors were more closely watched and were prevented from withholding 25 percent of the workers' wages until the end of the job, as they were accustomed to doing.

Miners and other nonfarm laborers had also turned to strikes in order to obtain improvements. Men of the Arizona copper mines called a strike in 1915 over the issue of the special rates usually paid to Mexican workers. This strike, like most others at the time, resulted in the strikers being arrested and ordered to "go home." Two years later, Mexican workers again called a strike in the Arizona copper mines. This time, they were shipped by train, in boxcars, to a New Mexico desert, where they were dumped out and abandoned.

In the 1930s, Mexicans were again involved in strike activities. In 1933, the Los Angeles local of the International Ladies Garment Workers Union (ILGWU) became the first union to strike under the National Recovery Act, which guaranteed the right to organize and bargain collectively. Half of the garment workers in the local union were Mexican-Americans. In 1936, another garment industry strike was called, and again Mexican women were in the forefront of picket activity.

The Bisbee copper mine in Arizona. During the early years of the 20th century, Mexican-American copper miners turned to strikes in an effort to improve wages.

World War II caused changes in the fight for economic opportunity. During the war years workers on the home front took skilled war-industry jobs, while men in the army mastered the skilled jobs of the military. After these experiences, Mexican-Americans could no longer accept the stereotype of "inferior race" or the label "foreigner." With their new self-image, they began the battle for improved working conditions with a new dedication.

Strikes called throughout the Southwest in 1946 exemplified this new spirit. Copper miners struck because companies were stalling on compliance with the orders of President Roosevelt's Fair Employment Practice Committee. The committee had ordered all companies to abandon their system of special discriminatory rates of pay. One of the leaders of this strike was Humberto Silex of El Paso. Prior to his part in the strike, Silex had organized a local of the International Union of Mine, Mill, and Smelter Workers in El Paso. As a result of his union and strike activities, Silex was arrested and deported. But this time the old familiar story had a new ending, for he later won his fight against the deportation order in the courts.

World War II also brought new economic problems for the Mexican-American. During the wartime emergency in 1942, the United States negotiated an agreement with Mexico for the importation of contract workers—*braceros*—who would work for a season and then be returned to Mexico. Mexican agents selected the men, and agents of the United States guaranteed decent housing and pay. Because the bracero program was needed to remedy a shortage of farm labor, it seemed quite acceptable during the war years. But after the war, the growers proclaimed a great need for additional labor, and the program was continued. In 1951, Congress formalized the agreement with Mexico by passing Public Law 78, under which 190,000 braceros were contracted within the year.

Though the bracero program continued, the needs of the growers were not satisfied. By offering employment to illegal immigrants (wetbacks), they could save a great deal of administrative work and substantial fees. Thousands of Mexican workers

Mexican authorities prepare a group of braceros for their journey to the United States.

also came on temporary visas, called green cards. Because the
green-carders lived on the Mexican side of the border, they
worked for lower wages and spent their incomes in Mexico,
where the cost of living was much less. Agriculture came to
depend on the wetbacks and green-carders, who didn't require
company benefits for sickness and retirement.

Mexican-American workers were hurt by competition with the
low-paid braceros, wetbacks, and green-carders. They needed
higher wages in order to live in the United States and to maintain
the American standard of living which they had acquired. By the
mid-fifties, the braceros also began to suffer. The growers did
not always live up to the promised standards of decent living
conditions. Having no rights or protections under American laws,
the braceros were often herded like cattle and worked like
animals. Mexico complained that the workers were faced with
local discrimination and at times refused to honor orders for
braceros, especially from communities in Texas and Arkansas.
The insistent United States farmers, however, pressured Mexico
into yielding each time. For the growers, the bracero program
had become a necessity.

The bracero and green-card programs enabled the United States government to institute the first real restrictions on illegal Mexican labor. Before these legal supplies of cheap labor were available, border state legislators had succeeded in keeping border patrol appropriations too low to support an effective patrol. Thus, wetbacks could easily slip over the border and supply needed labor. When the United States Immigration and Naturalization Service conducted "Operation Wetback" in 1954, this era came to an end. In one year over a million people were apprehended, and by the end of five years, a total of 3.8 million had been expelled.

Members of the United States Border Patrol follow the tracks of illegal immigrants in the hills near El Paso, Texas.

While the removal of a source of competition benefited the Mexican-American, Operation Wetback also caused many violations of civil rights. Hundreds of thousands of American citizens were stopped and questioned because they "looked Mexican." If the person stopped could not immediately produce documentary evidence of his legal status, he ran the risk of being sent "home" to Mexico. This form of harassment led to many deportations similar to those of the depression era.

The success of Operation Wetback brought about a decrease in the illegal labor supply, but at the same time it caused an increase in the number of braceros hired to work in the United

States. The American farm workers remained at an extreme disadvantage. According to 1955 statistics, farm workers were by far the lowest paid of any group of American workers. Hired farm labor averaged 58 cents an hour normally; during the peak harvest season the average was 68 cents an hour. The problem of a low hourly rate was compounded by the problem of finding steady work. Travel time was never paid for, nor were workers paid when the crops failed.

Agricultural workers fought to end the bracero programs which contributed to their economic problems. They argued that aliens reduced the number of jobs for citizens and lowered the pay rate. The bracero program, they pointed out, was unnecessary when millions of Americans were unemployed or underemployed. To them, it seemed to be a subsidy given to the handful of large corporate farmers who profited from the substandard wages. Countering these arguments, the employers claimed that there were not enough domestic workers and that native Americans were either unqualified for the stoop-labor jobs in the fields or less effective in performing them.

By 1960 the power of the growers had diminished, and Congress at last began to listen to organized labor and the Mexican-

Braceros waiting at a Mexican processing office. The bracero program provided a source of cheap labor for American agricultural employers, but it caused hardships for Mexican-American workers.

Americans. But it was not until December 31, 1964, that the bracero program finally ended. The Department of Labor ruled that, after the program's end, braceros could only be hired in the border towns, and that they would have to be paid $1.40 an hour. It also ruled that the local farm workers could no longer be paid less than the Mexican nationals who came to work in the fields.

The power of the railroads and the ranching and mining industries had also declined by the 1960s. These interests had encouraged a policy of unrestricted immigration from Mexico. During the 1950s, over 293,500 people had come to the United States, and the flow was increasing in the sixties. But the increase in immigration, combined with the decreasing influence of the railroad, ranching, and mining interests, caused Congressmen to be swayed by other factors. They listened to businessmen from the Northeast who saw no reason why they should help to provide their southwestern competitors with a supply of cheap labor. Together with welfare agencies and organized labor, the businessmen opposed the policy of unrestricted immigration.

The combined influences of these groups brought about the passage of the Immigration and Naturalization Act of 1965, which limited the number of immigrants from countries in the Western Hemisphere to 120,000 per year. This bill, which took effect in 1968, changed the characteristics of the immigration from Mexico. No longer were the majority of immigrants working males, but rather the wives and children of men already in the United States. In the years 1965 to 1969, at least 78 percent of the immigrants were women and children, as compared to the 50 percent who were women and children between 1955 and 1959.

The era of restrictions helped the cause of the Mexican-American in many ways. It reduced competition for jobs and allowed workers to organize effectively. No longer could a grower easily replace a field full of workers or threaten to deport those who demanded better working conditions and wages. Realizing that the time was ripe for change, Cesar Chávez led the fight to improve the economic situation of Mexican-Americans. Formerly a CSO organizer, Chávez had been involved in the struggle to end the bracero program and in other efforts on behalf of Mexican-American workers. In 1952 he led a march which helped to bring about a complete investigation of the Farm Placement Bureau. After forcing change in this organization, he went on to help the migrant worker in other ways. In 1962 he organized the National Farm Workers Association (NFWA), and by 1964 he had recruited 50,000 members into the union. That year NFWA took one employer to court for paying less than the minimum wage rate and, after months of wrangling, won the case. Encouraged by this victory, Chávez signed up a group of rose-grafters in 1965 and won a strike for higher wages. After only four days of the strike, the growers agreed to give the workers a 120 percent wage increase.

Later in 1965, Chávez undertook a much larger battle, one which would require many years of effort to win. In September of that year, the members of NFWA voted to join the strike of Filipino grape pickers against the growers in Delano, California. The fight for better wages and improved working conditions began when 2,000 workers left the fields. A boycott was started in 1967 to pressure the table-grape growers into signing the union contract. This boycott first applied only to the Giumarra Vineyards Corporation, the largest table-grape producer in the United States. After the company attempted sales under other names, however, the boycott was extended to all table grapes. Chávez appealed to all stores and consumers, asking them not to buy table grapes. The boycott became national and was also extended to Great Britain and Scandinavia. Grape sales fell 12 percent in 1968 and 15 percent in 1969. Influenced by the sales drop, a few growers agreed to bargain with the farm workers in 1969. Finally, in April 1970, a breakthrough came. After a five-year strike and a three-year boycott, the grape-pickers union won recognition in California and signed contracts with 85 percent of the state's table-grape growers.

The success of the grape pickers' strike, however, did not solve all the problems of the farm workers. Cesar Chávez soon turned his attention to lettuce workers and other farm laborers. Wage disputes continue today and many old problems remain. But new

A representative of the United Farm Workers Organizing Committee places his union's stamp of approval on crates of table grapes after the settlement of the grape pickers' strike in 1970.

problems also face the farm worker. Confronted with demands for better working conditions and higher salaries, more growers are turning to mechanized helpers. Machines have been perfected to pick tomatoes, cotton, and other products. Thousands of jobs in canneries and food-processing plants have also been eliminated by the new technology. Rather than improving conditions for workers, many employers are hiring fewer and fewer people.

The farm workers who remain in the fields are also beset by problems. Their living conditions are still among the worst in the country; the death rates in the migrant population are higher than the national average for other persons, and lack of food causes the average Mexican-American to live 10 years less than the average Anglo-American. Malnutrition among children is also a major problem; the instance of malnutrition is 10 times greater among migrant workers than among the nation's children generally. This malnutrition is serious enough to endanger mental development and stunt growth. Though there are guidelines and standards for migrant camps, part of the problem has been lack of enforcement and scarcity of inspectors.

Many solutions have been attempted in recent years to solve the problems, but so far none has significantly improved the lot of the migrant workers. In 1970 it was reported that the average income of the migrant families was only $2,021—less than half the federal poverty level for other families of the same size. Despite this statistic, fewer than 1 in 10 received welfare assistance of any kind. Migrant families are deprived of such aid primarily because of their mobility and their ignorance of available benefits. Bureaucratic conflicts also make it difficult for them to get welfare assistance.

In March 1971, President Richard Nixon attempted to aid the migrant worker by extending the concept of disaster relief to include aid to migrant workers left unemployed as a result of crop failures. (Disaster aid includes unemployment compensation and food stamps.) It was hoped that this move will minimize the effects of natural disasters on the migrants' income.

Another governmental attempt to aid the migrant has been the federal suit filed in 1971 against a farm owner in Van Buren

Migrant laborers often live under conditions of extreme poverty.

County, Michigan, the area which has the largest concentration of migrant workers in the United States. Each year, between May and September, more than 21,000 workers, mostly Mexican-American, harvest fruit and vegetable crops there. The suit claims that migrants are being deprived of information about aid programs open to them because representatives of the various federal, state, local, and private assistance programs are kept from entering the camps.

On June 20, 1971, another action was taken by the federal government, this one more controversial than the previous two. On that day Labor Secretary James D. Hodgson announced a $20-million manpower program for migrant laborers. He stated that the funds would be in addition to the regular budget for the Farm Labor Service. The money would provide health care, educational assistance, food stamps, and housing services. In addition, training and job development would be provided for seasonal workers who wanted to leave the migrant work force.

The manpower program, according to Secretary Hodgson, would help more than 6,000 migrant workers attain economic independence and security, and prepare them for year-round employment. However, the program was denounced by several migrant groups. They objected to the Farm Labor Service being in charge of the program, pointing out that a Labor Department investigation had found the service to be guilty of discrimination. The service has also been criticized recently for being a grower-staffed and grower-oriented network that cycles migrants into poverty. Migrant groups claim that it now functions to guarantee growers a cheap supply of labor. These groups feel that the farm worker ought to have an opportunity to run his own manpower program, rather than to have a program run by the Farm Labor Service.

Severe as the problems of farm laborers are today, however, they are actually only a small portion of the economic problems that face Mexican-Americans. Most of the problem is actually an urban one, since 72 percent of the poor among Mexican-Americans are city dwellers. From one-third to one-half of the Mexican-American population live below the official level of poverty, or immediately above it. Mexican-American families have an income which is 65 percent that of Anglo-American families. Because Mexican-American families are large, their per-person income is less than half that of Anglos.

Though the problems are fairly clear, the solutions do not seem to be so obvious. In the past, attempts have been made to curb the unfair competition of Mexican workers who entered the United States legally or illegally. Today, however, Mexican nationals continue to be a problem for Mexican-Americans engaged in domestic work. In the border cities, thousands of Mexican workers commute to their jobs in the United States each morning, returning to Mexico each evening. This arrangement has advantages and disadvantages for both countries. Mexico benefits by the employment of its people and by the dollars that they bring back. The United States benefits by the low wages paid to the Mexican worker and by the money which they leave behind in return for American merchandise. At the same time, however, commuting workers lower wages and take away jobs from American citizens. In addition, they hamper the American workers' effort to organize.

Another recurring problem is that of the wetback. Currently there are an estimated 1 million Mexican workers who have entered this country illegally. They are encouraged to come by the ease with which they can cross the border and avoid punishment as well. As in the past, these illegal entries undercut American job seekers. In 1970, the effort to halt this flow of labor was again increased; the United States Immigration and Naturalization Service caught over 317,000 illegal aliens in that year. A new bill before Congress would attempt to stop the inflow of wetbacks in yet another way. Criminal penalties would be imposed upon United States citizens who employ such illegal aliens. If passed, the measure would radically alter the current laws regarding wetbacks. The existing laws punish those who "harbor" or "conceal" an illegal worker, but not those who hire him. The proposed change in the law would have a drastic effect on those employers who have come to depend on a cheap labor source.

5. *A New Sense of Pride*

The Chicano population in the United States is steadily growing and in the years from 1971 to 1979 comprised nearly 15 percent of all U.S. immigrants. The approximately 7.5 million Mexican-Americans in the United States today make up more than 4 percent of the nation's population. Two southwestern states—California and Texas—are home to more than 75 percent of all Mexican Americans. Today, at least 80 percent live in urban areas, the majority in barrios. More Mexican-Americans live in Los Angeles than in any other city in the nation. The second largest concentration of Mexican-Americans is in San Antonio, Texas—the nation's 10th largest city.

The Mexican-American people still maintain many cultural traditions from the past, although each generation preserves fewer of them. Some of the most important traditions are those connected with the Catholic Church, for instance, the celebration of the Saint's Day feast and other religious holidays. Familiar

Mexican foods and music have also been retained, and of course Spanish is still spoken by most Mexican-Americans. The traditional values of respectful conduct, obedience, and pride are important to Mexican-Americans today, as is the tradition of *machismo*, or manliness.

In recent years, Mexican-Americans have gained a new pride in their identity and cultural heritage. The name "Mexican" is now respected, and many who had left the Mexican-American communities are returning to them and acknowledging their heritage. *La Causa*, the advancement of Mexican-Americans, has become a central theme in the lives of many Chicanos. The name "Chicano" itself is becoming popular, as are the mottos "Chicano Power" and "Bronze is beautiful." But Mexican-Americans, now as in the past, differ widely in attitudes, political beliefs, and social positions. While some are turning to radical isolationism, others are finding acceptance in the majority community.

Today, however, the goal of most Chicanos is no longer merely one of acceptance. The proud people who built the Southwest and who contributed so much to American life now insist that the truth about their contributions be recognized and their unique heritage be respected. Rather than seeking to abandon their identity, they now ask to be accepted as both a bilingual and a bicultural people.

PART IV

Individuals
and Their Achievements

A number of outstanding Mexican-Americans have won national recognition and acclaim in recent years. Through their achievements in the areas of government, community leadership, literature, scholarship, sports, and entertainment, they have made an important contribution to American life.

1. *Ambassadors*

Born in El Paso, Texas, Raymond L. Telles gained political importance as the mayor of El Paso (1957-61) and as the United States ambassador to Costa Rica (1961-67). Telles has served as an ambassador to the United States-Mexico Commission of Border Development and Friendship, and he has been commissioner of the Equal Employment Opportunity Commission in Washington, D.C., since 1971.

Benigno C. Hernandez, a native of New Mexico, was the ambassador to Paraguay from 1967 to 1969. He has been involved in numerous civic activities in Albuquerque, where he lives, including serving as chairman of the Albuquerque Citizens Committee. He is also a judge on the New Mexico Court of Appeals in Santa Fe.

Born in Cananea, Mexico, Raul Hector Castro moved to the United States in 1926 and became a naturalized citizen in 1939. A successful Arizona lawyer, Castro served as ambassador to El Salvador (1964-68) and Bolivia (1968-69). After one term as the governor of Arizona (1975-77), Castro was appointed ambassador to Argentina in 1977. He died in 1980.

Philip V. Sanchez, former director of the Office of Economic Opportunity (1971-73), was ambassador to Honduras from 1973

Benigno C. Hernandez, former United States ambassador to Paraguay, presents a diploma to a Paraguayan teacher.

to 1976. When this small Central American country was struck by a devastating hurricane in 1974, Ambassador Sanchez directed the United States emergency relief program. Sanchez was later ambassador to Columbia (1976-77).

John Gavin, appointed U.S. ambassador to Mexico in 1981, was an actor before turning to politics. From 1961 to 1974, he served as the Special Advisor to the Secretariet General Organization of American States, and he was spokesman for Bank of America from 1973 to 1980.

2. *Elected and Appointed Officials*

In recent years, Mexican-Americans have been elected to public office in increasing numbers. Among the Chicanos holding important political offices are several distinguished members of the United States Congress and governors of two Southwestern states.

Henry B. Gonzalez, representative from Texas, holds the distinction of being the first Mexican-American to be sent to the United States Congress. Gonzalez was first elected to public office in 1953, when he became a member of the city council in San Antonio, Texas. Three years later he was elected to the

Henry B. Gonzalez   Eligio de la Garza

Texas state senate, thus becoming the first Mexican-American to be seated in that body in 110 years.

Gonzalez's greatest political triumph came in 1961, when he was elected to the 87th Congress as a representative from Texas. Repeatedly reelected to Congress, Gonzalez has worked hard for many goals, including benefits for farm workers, better education and housing for the poor, and the minimum wage. His most important legislative accomplishment to date has been the defeat of the bracero program, which ended on December 31, 1964.

Edward R. Roybal, California representative in Congress, was born in Albuquerque, New Mexico. Political recognition first came for Roybal in 1947, when he decided to run for the city council in Los Angeles. Since 1881, no Mexican-American had succeeded in winning a seat on the council. To promote his election, Roybal and a committee of his supporters organized what later became known as the Community Service Organization.

Although Roybal lost the 1947 election, he ran again in the 1949 election and won. Reelected for three additional terms, Roybal served on the Los Angeles City Council for over 12 years. Then, in 1962, Roybal was elected to the United States House of Representatives. A Democrat, the California congressman has been active on both the Appropriations Committee and the Foreign Affairs Committee.

A third Mexican-American to be elected to the United States

House of Representatives is Eligio "Kika" de la Garza. Born in Mercedes, Texas, he has had one of the most notable careers of all the Chicanos now seated in Congress. After serving six consecutive two-year terms as a member of the Texas House of Representatives, de la Garza was elected to Congress in 1964. Two years later he served as a member of the United States delegation to the Mexico-United States Inter-Parliamentary Union at Washington, D.C. He was a delegate to the same conference in 1967 and in 1968.

Reelected to the House of Representatives several times, de la Garza has been an active member of both the Agricultural Committee and the Merchant Marine and Fisheries Committee. Congressman de la Garza is also a member of the League of United Latin American Citizens, and has worked hard to further the cause of the Mexican-Americans.

Also serving in the United States Congress is Manuel Lujan, Jr., a Republican representing the first congressional district of New Mexico. Born near the San Ildefonso Indian Pueblo in northern New Mexico, Lujan was active in community affairs in Santa Fe and Albuquerque before his election to the House of Representatives in 1968. As a congressman, Lujan has taken an active interest in legislation to improve education on the state level and to provide bilingual educational programs.

The late Joseph Montoya was the first Mexican-American to become a United States senator. A native of New Mexico, Montoya was elected to that state's house of representatives in 1936. Only 21 years old at the time, Montoya was the youngest man ever to be seated on New Mexico's state legislature. In 1938 he was reelected to the New Mexico House of Representatives and named the majority floor leader.

Montoya, a Democrat, was elected to the New Mexico state senate in 1940. Six years later he was elected as lieutenant governor of New Mexico, and in 1957 as one of New Mexico's representatives to the 85th United States Congress. Montoya's most important political victory came in 1964, when he was first elected to the United States Senate.

During the next 12 years, Senator Montoya was actively

involved in the civil rights movement, in consumer legislation, and in legislation calling for an end to the Vietnam War. Montoya came to national attention in 1973 when he was appointed to the Senate Watergate committee, which eventually uncovered the Watergate scandal involving President Richard Nixon and his top aides. Senator Montoya was defeated for reelection in 1976. He died two years later.

Americans of Mexican ancestry have also served in state government. Ex-ambassador Raul Hector Castro was the Democratic governor of Arizona from 1975 to 1977. From 1975 to 1979, Democrat Jerry Apodaca was governor of New Mexico, and earlier he had served as the state senator from Las Cruces (1966-74). An avid jogger, Apodaca was appointed chairman of the President's Council on Physical Fitness in 1978. In California, Mario Obledo is secretary of health and welfare in Governor Jerry Brown's administration. Governor Brown has also appointed 27 Mexican-American judges to state office.

Two prominent Mexican-American federal office holders are Leonel J. Castillo and Graciela Olivarez. Castillo is the first Hispanic commissioner of the Immigration and Naturalization Service. The grandson of an illegal immigrant, he grew up in the Galveston-Houston area. Before being appointed INS commissioner in 1977, Castillo worked with various Texas community poverty projects, served in the Peace Corps in the Philippines, and was Houston's controller. Graciela Olivarez, director of the federal Community Services Administration, was the first woman to graduate from the University of Notre Dame Law School.

3. Community Leaders

Many Mexican-Americans have gained recognition as leaders of the Chicano community. Although their methods have varied, they have all been dedicated to advancing the cause of their people.

A one-time grape picker from an impoverished background, Cesar Chávez organized the National Farm Workers Association in 1962 so that California farm laborers could bargain with farm owners and growers for better wages and working conditions.

Cesar Chávez signs an agreement between striking grape pickers and grape growers in 1970.

Three years later he initiated the historic grape pickers' strike against California grape growers. To increase the pressure on the growers, Chávez spearheaded a nationwide grape boycott in 1967. In 1970, Chávez triumphed, signing new contracts with over three-fourths of California's grape growers. Today Chávez is the president of the United Farm Workers of America.

Like Cesar Chávez, Rudolfo "Corky" Gonzales is a powerful leader of the Chicano community. Gonzales organized the Crusade for Justice in Denver, Colorado, in 1965. Through this militant organization, Gonzales is trying to achieve the social and economic betterment of his people. He also wants to prevent Chicanos from assimilating with their Anglo neighbors; this, he believes, could lead to a loss of their cultural heritage and identity.

In 1969 Gonzales and the Crusade for Justice hosted a week-long Chicano Youth Liberation Conference in Denver. During this conference the Spiritual Plan of Aztlan was adopted (Aztlan was the name of the ancient Aztec nation). In this document the Chicanos defined their historical heritage, reclaimed the land of their birth (the Southwest), and declared themselves an independent nation. The following year Gonzales organized another Chicano Youth Liberation Conference. This time, he proposed that a Congress of Aztlan be established to start programs of economic development, an independent Chicano school system, free Chicano universities, and community health programs.

The son of a sharecropper, Reies Tijerina has been one of the most militant and controversial leaders of the Chicano community. Born in Falls City, Texas, Tijerina traveled to New Mexico in 1963 to organize the Alianza Federal de Mercedes. Now known as the Alianza Federal de los Pueblos Libres, the organization is attempting to help Mexican-Americans regain millions of acres of land in the Southwest. This land was granted to their ancestors by Spanish kings and the Mexican government, and was illegally seized by Anglo-Americans. Tijerina claims that since these land grants were guaranteed by the Treaty of Guadalupe-Hidalgo in 1848, they must be returned to their rightful owners — the Chicanos.

In January 1970 Tijerina began serving a prison sentence after he was found guilty of charges stemming from his participation in a 1967 armed raid on a New Mexico courthouse. He was paroled in May of 1971. Although the conditions of his parole forced Tijerina to resign as president of the Alianza, he still

Reies Tijerina speaks to supporters after his release from prison in 1971.

supports the organization's goals. He has made it clear, however, that these goals do not include establishing an independent Chicano nation in the Southwest. Instead, Tijerina would like to bring Chicanos together with their Anglo neighbors.

Several other community leaders have gained more recent attention. Raul Yzaguirre is director of the National Council of *La Raza* (The Race), a group encompassing many Hispanic-American organizations. A former activist with *La Raza Unida* (The United Race), Willie Velasquez heads the San Antonio-based Southwest Voter Registration Education Project. Vilma Martinez, president of the Mexican-American Legal Defense and Education Fund (MALDEF), was appointed by Governor Brown to the board of regents of the University of California.

4. *Writers*

In addition to their political and community activities, the Mexican-Americans have made significant contributions in the area of literature. Among the talented Chicano writers who have emerged are the playwright Luis Valdez, the poet Augustín Lira, and the novelist Richard Vasquez.

The Chicano theater group El Teatro Campesino performs in Mexico City, 1972.

Luis Valdez

The founder of *El Teatro Campesino* (the Farm Workers Theater), playwright Luis Valdez has played a major role in the cultural awakening of the Southwest. Valdez established the Farm Workers Theater in Delano, California, in 1965—just two months after the historic grape pickers' strike had begun there. The theater was composed entirely of farm workers, and the vineyards served as its stage. Within a few years, *El Teatro Campesino* won national recognition and led to the establishment of similar Chicano theaters throughout the Southwest. *Zoot Suit* (1978), one of Valdez's most successful plays, dramatized the Los Angeles race riots of 1942-43.

Abelardo Delgado, Benjamin Luan, Guadalupe de Saavedra, Augustín Lira—these are but a few of the Mexican-Americans who have proven themselves as poets in recent years. The work of Augustín Lira is representative of the poetry of the new group of Chicano poets. While his poems reflect the pain and sorrow of the Mexican-Americans, they also reflect his people's growing hope and pride.

The Mexican-Americans have found yet another voice in the Chicano novelist Richard Vasquez. A newspaperman, publicist, and screenwriter, Vasquez's first novel was published in 1970. Entitled *Chicano*, the novel is a powerful narrative of life in the Mexican-American barrios of East Los Angeles.

5. *Scholars*

The long list of Chicano scholars and professors is as impressive as the list of Chicano writers. Ernesto Galarza, Octavio Romano,

Pancho Gonzales   **Jim Plunkett**   **Lee Trevino**

Manuel Guerra, José Roberto Juarez, Feliciano Rivera, and George Sanchez are just a few of the Mexican-Americans who have distinguished themselves in the area of scholarship.

Representative of the group is Ernesto Galarza, who has been called the "dean" of the Chicano leaders and the "grandfather of the Chicano movement." A man of many talents, Galarza has won esteem as a teacher, a sociologist, and a writer. *Merchants of Labor,* a book on Mexican-American migrant workers, is one of his most important works.

6. *Sports Figures*

The Mexican-Americans have also excelled in the field of sports. Just as Rudolfo "Corky" Gonzales won national recognition and acclaim as a champion boxer, Richard Gonzales, Joe Kapp, Jim Plunkett, Fernando Venezuela, Lee Trevino, and Nancy Lopez have won recognition in such fields as tennis, football, baseball and golf.

Richard "Pancho" Gonzales has been called one of the greatest tennis players of the 20th century. A self-taught player, "Pancho" became a national celebrity in 1948 by winning the United States Tennis Championship. Gonzales, only 20, was one of the youngest players ever to win the event. He was also one of the few players to hold the turf, clay, and indoor championships at the same time. In 1970 he enjoyed one of the most important victories of his two-decade career by defeating Rod Laver, the country's number one player at the time.

Joe Kapp and Jim Plunkett are two Chicanos who have won fame as football players. Joe Kapp played as quarterback with two NFL teams— the New England Patriots and the Minnesota Vikings—during his career. In 1969 he was voted the Second Most Valuable Player of the NFL. When Kapp left the New England Patriots in 1971, he was replaced by another outstanding Chicano quarterback, Jim Plunkett. Plunkett, who won the Heisman Trophy in 1970 and was named the AFC Rookie of the Year in 1971, later played for the San Francisco 49ers (1976-77). In 1978 he signed with the Oakland Raiders and went on to be voted the Most Valuable Player of the 1979 Super Bowl.

Born in Sonora, Mexico, in 1960, Fernando Venezuela joined the Los Angeles Dodgers late in 1980. His outstanding pitching record helped the Dodgers to capture the 1981 World Series title. Venezuela was the recipient of the 1981 Cy Young Award.

Champion golfer Lee Trevino rose to international fame in 1968 by winning his first United State Open title. "Super Mex," as Trevino calls himself, was the leading money and point winner in professional golf in 1970. Trevino made golf history the following year by winning not only his second United States Open title, but both the Canadian Open and British Open titles as well. He was also named the PGA Player of the Year. In 1972 Trevino won his second British Open title, and in 1974 he captured his first PGA championship and the World Series Golf title. After a 15-month winless stretch, Trevino won his second Canadian Open title in 1977.

Another gifted Chicano golfer is Nancy Lopez, who had a remarkable career in amateur golf before turning pro in 1977. Lopez, who started playing when she was only eight years old, won the USGA Junior Girls title in 1974 at age 17. One year later, she finished second in the United States Open. After winning the national collegiate title in 1976, Lopez turned professional and was the runner-up in the 1977 U.S. Women's

Open Golf Championship. In 1978 Lopez entered 21 events and won 8, including the Ladies' PGA Championship.

7. *Entertainers*

As in sports, Mexican-Americans have done well in the entertainment world. Trini Lopez, Vikki Carr, Linda Ronstadt, Joan Baez, Ricardo Montalban, and Anthony Quinn have entertained millions with their fine performances.

Singer-guitarist Trini Lopez was born Trinidad Lopez III in Dallas, Texas. To date, he has sold millions of records, has entertained in nightclubs across the country, and has starred in two motion pictures. "If I Had a Hammer," "Lemon Tree," and "Michael—Row the Boat Ashore" have been among his biggest hits.

Born Florencia Bisenta de Casillas Martinez Cardona Moss in El Paso, Texas, Vikki Carr started singing during her high school years and gained fame as a singer with Pepe Callahan's Mexican-Irish band. Today Vikki Carr is one of the finest vocalists in the United States, appearing on countless TV programs and in nightclubs around the world. In November 1967 she gave a Royal

Trini Lopez is a talented Mexican-American singer and guitarist.

Vikki Carr   Joan Baez

Command Performance before Queen Elizabeth II in London. She was given the "Outstanding Entertainer of the Year" award by the Mexican-American Council of California in 1968 and, in 1981, received the Humanitarian Award Nosotros. Some of Carr's most popular songs include "For Once in My Life," "It Must Be Him," "I'll Be on My Way, " and "The First Time Ever I Saw Your Face."

Linda Ronstadt, who is of Mexican and German descent, is one of today's most popular female vocalists. Born in Tucson, Arizona, she has had five platinum albums and has won two Grammy Awards.

Another talented Mexican-American vocalist is folk singer Joan Baez. Born on New York's Staten Island, Baez got her start by singing in college coffeehouses. In 1959 the singer was an instant hit at the Newport Folk Festival in Rhode Island, and from there she went on to become a national celebrity. She appeared in Carnegie Hall in 1962 and since has made concert tours throughout the United States and abroad.

A political liberal, Joan Baez is also known for her protest activities. She has marched—for civil rights, for student rights, and for the end of the Vietnam war—and in 1965 she founded the Resource Center for Non-Violence. Baez also served on the national advisory committee for Amnesty International in 1974 and, in 1979, was president of Humanitas/International human rights committee. With her husband, David, she co-authored the book *Daybreak* in 1968, and in 1971 she wrote a second book, *Coming Out.*.

As in music, Chicanos have distinguished themselves in motion pictures. Several Mexican-American actors have played "Latin Lovers" on the screen including Ramon Novarro, Gilbert Roland, and Ricardo Montalban.

Actor Ricardo Montalban, born in Mexico City, first appeared in Mexican pictures. Later he came to the United States and began his long career as one of Hollywood's handsomest leading men. Montalban has appeared in dozens of films, including *The Kissing Bandit, Latin Lovers, Sayonara,* and *Sweet Charity,* and on television. His popular TV series, *Fantasy Island,* was first shown in 1978.

Actor Anthony Quinn has won both national and international acclaim for his motion picture performances. The actor, born in 1915 in Chihuahua, Mexico, during the Mexican revolution, was smuggled out of Mexico to Los Angeles by his mother.

Quinn began his Hollywood film career in 1935 by starring with Mae West in *Clean Beds.* Since then Anthony Quinn has appeared in more than 100 films, has won two Oscars as Best Supporting Actor, and has won several Academy Award nominations as Best Actor. Quinn is best known for his performance in *Zorba the Greek* (1964). In addition to acting, Quinn has written both movie scripts and novels. His first book, *The Original Sin,* was published in 1972.

Great Depression, 41-42
green-carders, 72-73
Guadalupe-Hidalgo, Treaty of, 22-23, 25, 26, 59, 67
Guadalupe, Virgin of, 13
Guerra, Manuel, 92
Gutierrez, José, 56

Hernandez, Benigno C., 83, 84
Hidalgo y Costilla, Miguel, 18
Houston, Sam, 22

Immigration Act of 1924, 30, 37, 41
Immigration and Naturalization Act of 1965, 75
Imperial Valley, 30
Inter-Agency on Mexican American Affairs, 57
International Ladies Garment Workers Union (ILGWU), 70
Isabella (queen of Spain), 10, 17-18

Juarez, José Roberto, 92

Kapp, Joe, 92, 93

League of United Latin American Citizens (LULAC), 51, 61
Lira, Augustín, 90, 91
Little School of the 400, 61-62
Lopez, Nancy, 92, 93
Lopez, Trini, 94
Lujan, Manuel, Jr., 86
Luan, Benjamin, 91

machismo, 82
Malinche, 10
Marcos de Niza, 14
Martinez, Vilma, 90
mestizos, 12, 13, 14, 16
Mexican American Political Association (MAPA), 54, 55, 56
Mexican-Americans: educational level of, 65-66; income of, 79-80; other names used by, 7, 51; population distribution of, 79, 81; relation to Mexico of, 7
Mexican American Student Conference (MASC), 65

Mexican American Student Organization (MASO), 65
Mexican-American War, 22
Mexican American Youth Organization (MAYO), 56, 65
Mexico, 9; civil war in, 29, 33; conquest of, 10-12; independence of, 18; and war with the United States, 22
Migrant Children Educational Assistance Act of 1960, 65
migrant labor camps, 31-32, 77-78
migrant workers, 30-32, 65, 69, 74, 77-79
mining in the Southwest, 24-25, 28, 32
missions, 14, 15, 16, 17, 18
Moctezuma II, 9, 10-11
Montalban, Ricardo, 94, 96
Montez, Philip, 58
Montoya, Joseph, 86-87
Moreno, John, 54
Movimento Estudiantil Chicano de Aztlán (MECHA), 65
Murieta, Joaquin, 27
mutualistas, 51

National Farm Workers Association (NFWA), 76
National Organization of Mexican American Students (NOMAS), 65
New Spain, 12-13, 15, 17-18
(La) Noche Triste, 11
Novarro, Ramon, 95

Obledo, Mario, 87
Olivarez, Graciela, 87
Oñate, Juan de, 14
Operation Wetback, 73
peninsulares, 13, 16, 18
peons, 33
personalissmo, 21
Plunkett, Jim, 92, 93
police brutality, 66
Political Association of Spanish Speaking Organizations (PASSO), 54-55
presidio, 14-16
Public Law 78, 71
pueblo, 14-15, 17
Pueblo Indians, revolt of, 14
pueblo laws, 17

Quetzalcoatl, 10
Quinn, Anthony, 94, 96
quotas, immigration, 37, 39

railroads, 28, 29
Ramirez, Lorenzo, 58
ranching in the Southwest, 19, 24, 26
(La) Raza, 51
(La) Raza Unida Conference, 56
(La) Raza Unida Party, 56
Reclamation Act of 1902, 28
"repatriation" of Mexicans, 42-44
Rivera, Diego, 42
Rivera, Feliciano, 92
Rodriguez, Armando, 58
Rodriguez, Tony, 58
Roland, Gilbert, 95
Roman Catholic Church, 10, 12-13, 19,
    21, 81
Romano, Octavio, 91
Ronstadt, Linda, 94, 95
Roybal, Edward, 54, 85
Ruiz, Manuel, Jr., 58

Saavedra, Guadalupe de, 91
Salazar, Ruben, 66
Sanchez, David, 66
Sanchez, George, 92
Sanchez, Manuel, 58
Sanchez, Philip, 58, 83-84
Sandoval, Hilary, 58
Santa Anna, Antonio López de, 21-22
Sante Fe, 14, 16
Scott, Winfield, 22
Serra, Junípero, 15
Silex, Humberto, 71
Sleepy Lagoon case, 47-48
Small Business Administration (SBA),
    58
Soto, Philip, 54
Southwest Council of La Raza, 56-57
Spanish language, 7, 19, 24, 25-26, 60,
    62, 82
strikes, 69-71, 76
sugar beets, 30, 41

Taylor, Zachary, 22
(El) Teatro Campesino, 90-91
Telles, Raymond L., 83
Tenochtitlán, 9, 10-12
Texas: Anglo settlements in, 20-21;
    annexation of, 22; conflicts between
    Anglos and Mexicans in, 20-21;
    exploration of, 14
Texas Emigrant Agent Law, 41
Tijerina, Reies, 56, 67-68, 89-90
Trevino, Lee, 92, 93

unions, 69-70, 76
United Farm Workers of America, 88
United Mexican American Students
    (UMAS), 65
U.S. Immigration and Naturalization
    Service, 73, 80
Unity Leagues, 52

Valdez, Luis, 90, 91
Vargas, Diego de, 14-15
Vasquez, Richard, 90, 91
Vasquez, Tiburcio, 27
Velasquez, Willie, 90
Venezuela, Fernando, 92, 93
voter registration, 52

wetbacks, 38, 71, 72, 73, 80
World War I, 32
World War II, 46, 50-51, 52, 71

Ximenes, Vicente T., 57-58

Yzaguirre, Raul, 90

zoot-suit riots, 48-49

The IN AMERICA *Series*

AMERICAN IMMIGRATION
The AMERICAN INDIAN *in America, Vol. I*
The AMERICAN INDIAN *in America, Vol. II*
The ARMENIANS *in America*
The BLACKS *in America*
The CHINESE *in America*
The CZECHS & SLOVAKS *in America*
The DUTCH *in America*
The EAST INDIANS & PAKISTANIS *in America*
The ENGLISH *in America*
The FINNS *in America*
The FRENCH *in America*
The GERMANS *in America*
The GREEKS *in America*
The HUNGARIANS *in America*
The IRISH *in America*
The ITALIANS *in America*
The JAPANESE *in America*
The JEWS *in America*
The KOREANS *in America*
The MEXICANS *in America*
The NORWEGIANS *in America*
The POLES *in America*
The PUERTO RICANS *in America*
The RUSSIANS *in America*
The SCOTS & SCOTCH-IRISH *in America*
The SWEDES *in America*
The UKRAINIANS *in America*
The YUGOSLAVS *in America*
The FREEDOM OF THE PRESS *in America*
The FREEDOM OF RELIGION *in America*
The FREEDOM OF SPEECH *in America*

Lerner Publications Company
241 First Avenue North, Minneapolis, Minnesota 55401